Weather & Hazards

Michael Raw

Advanced
Topic*Master*

Philip Allan Updates, an imprint of Hodder Education, an Hachette UK company, Market Place, Deddington, Oxfordshire OX15 0SE

Orders
Bookpoint Ltd, 130 Milton Park, Abingdon, Oxfordshire OX14 4SB
tel: 01235 827720
fax: 01235 400454
e-mail: uk.orders@bookpoint.co.uk
Lines are open 9.00 a.m.–5.00 p.m., Monday to Saturday, with a 24-hour message answering service. You can also order through the Philip Allan Updates website: www.philipallan.co.uk

ISBN 978-1-4441-0833-0

First printed 2010
Impression number 5 4 3 2 1
Year 2014 2013 2012 2011 2010

Printed in Spain

Hachette UK's policy is to use papers that are natural, renewable and recyclable products and made from wood grown in sustainable forests. The logging and manufacturing processes are expected to conform to the environmental regulations of the country of origin

P01717

Contents

Introduction..3

Processes

1 The global energy system...4

The structure of the atmosphere.................................4

The global energy budget...5

The general circulation of the atmosphere.................9

2 Frost, fog and cloud 14

Phase changes and latent heat...................................14

Atmospheric humidity..15

Atmospheric moisture near the surface.....................17

Atmospheric moisture above the surface...................25

3 Precipitation...31

Definition..31

Formation of rain...31

Other forms of precipitation...33

Intensity and duration of precipitation events.........34

Precipitation types...35

4 Pressure and winds..39

Atmospheric pressure...39

Winds...41

5 Air masses...46

Origin and characteristics of air masses 46

Classification of air masses...46

Weather systems

6 Small- and medium-scale weather systems 51
  Dust devils 51
  Tornadoes 52
  Thunderstorms 55

7 Large-scale weather systems 59
  Depressions 59
  Tropical cyclones 63
  Anticyclones 70

Weather hazards

8 Thunderstorms, tornadoes and extreme weather hazards 74
  Hazardous weather events 74
  Thunderstorm hazards 75
  Hailstorm hazards 78
  Tornado hazards 82

9 Depressions and related weather hazards 86
  Heavy rainfall and flood hazards 86
  Storm surge and gale-force wind hazards 91
  Heavy snowfall and blizzard hazards 94

10 Tropical cyclone hazards 97
  Related hazards 97
  Flooding and mass movement hazards related to Hurricane Mitch 98
  Responding to tropical cyclone hazards 99
  Measuring and monitoring tropical cyclones 100
  Increasing frequency of hurricane activity 109
  The El Niño Southern Oscillation and weather patterns 110

11 Anticyclones and weather hazards 111
  Drought 111
  Wildfires in California 116
  Heatwave in Europe: August 2003 119
  Killer heatwaves and cities 122
  The UK's big chill: cold spell 2009–10 122

Introduction

Few areas of geography are more relevant to the interaction between people and the physical environment than the subject of weather and related hazards. Apart from its academic importance, this is a subject of enormous interest in our daily lives. Weather-related events, from blizzards to heatwaves, frequently make the news headlines, while interest in weather among Britons amounts to a national obsession. Extreme weather events elsewhere in the world are widely reported in the media and, with the growth of international travel, also have an increasing relevance to our lives.

This book has been written primarily for AS and A2 geography students, though it should also be useful to first-year undergraduates following geography, environmental science and related courses. Weather and climate hazards is a popular topic in most, if not all, 16–19 geography specifications. For example, AQA offers an A2 option on weather and climate hazards; Edexcel has an A2 option on extreme weather; and climate hazards figure as A2 options in the OCR and WJEC specifications. Other specifications, including CCEA, IB and pre-U, also have options in this subject area.

Although not explicitly structured in the text, this book should be considered in three parts. The first part covers Chapters 1 to 5 and deals with the atmospheric processes that generate weather. This provides essential background to the second part on weather systems in Chapters 6 and 7. Finally, Chapters 8 to 11 bring together physical and human systems through the investigation of weather hazards and their impact on people and society. Although in places connections are made between extreme weather and contemporary global climate change, the subject of global climate change per se is for the most part beyond the scope of this book.

Consistent with other books in the Advanced TopicMaster series, *Weather & Hazards* aims to challenge you and encourage you to extend your study beyond the strict boundaries of specifications. This is done not only through introducing more advanced topics such as jet streams, sea-surface temperatures and supercells, but also through activities which invite investigation and research, mainly through exploring the wealth of weather and climate data available on websites operated by NOAA, NASA, the Met Office and other national weather and climate agencies.

Michael Raw

1 The global energy system

The structure of the atmosphere

The Earth's atmosphere is the thin envelope of gases that surrounds the planet (Figure 1.1). It extends for over 100 km above the surface, though its density above 30 km is very low. In cross-section, the atmosphere is made up of a series of layers defined by the behaviour of temperature with height. In the lowest layer, known as the **troposphere**, temperatures decrease with height.

Figure 1.1	The vertical structure of the atmosphere

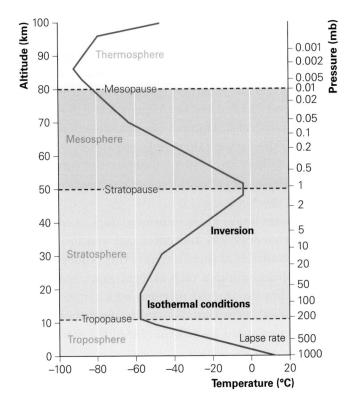

Table 1.1 Average composition of the atmosphere below 25 km (%)*

Nitrogen (N_2)	78.08
Oxygen (O_2)	20.94
Carbon dioxide (CO_2)	0.03 (variable)
Ozone (O_3)	0.000006

*Excluding water vapour

This lapse rate of temperature (see Chapter 2) averages $6.5\,°C\,km^{-1}$. In the **stratosphere**, we find the opposite situation, with temperatures increasing with height. This phenomenon is called a temperature **inversion**.

The troposphere accounts for three-quarters of the atmosphere's mass and varies in height from 6–8 km at the poles to 16–18 km at the equator. The troposphere also contains nearly all weather phenomena as we know them, including clouds, precipitation and winds.

The gaseous composition of the atmosphere is fairly constant with height. Nitrogen and oxygen account for 99% of the atmosphere by volume (Table 1.1). However, other gases, especially water vapour and carbon dioxide, although present in only small quantities, have a huge influence on weather and climate. Water vapour is particularly important. It plays a key role in cloud formation, precipitation and the Earth's energy budget. And yet on average it accounts for only 4% of the atmosphere by volume near the surface and is largely absent above 10 km.

The global energy budget

At the global scale, the Earth and the atmosphere form an energy system. The Earth–atmosphere system is an **open system** with inputs and outputs of both energy and matter. However, in reality, it is energy inputs and outputs that dominate the system: apart from incoming meteorites and outgoing space probes, transfers of matter across the system boundaries are negligible.

Energy inputs

Insolation (i.e. **in**coming **sol**ar rad**iation**) drives the global energy system. The sun is the source of this radiant energy, which consists of electromagnetic waves. Because the sun is a hot body (surface temperature 5000 °C) its radiant energy is mainly shortwave and concentrated in the visible part of

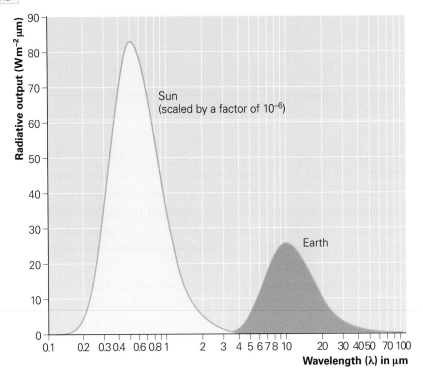

Figure 1.2 Radiation outputs from the sun and the Earth

the spectrum (Figure 1.2). Moreover, the atmosphere is largely transparent to insolation, with only a small fraction of short-wave radiation absorbed by gases in the atmosphere.

Less than half of all insolation reaches the Earth's surface and is converted to heat energy (Figure 1.3). The main loss is due to **reflection** by clouds. Short-wave radiation striking cloud tops bounces back into space without being converted into heat. Losses also occur at the Earth's surface, especially from highly reflective surfaces such as snow and ice (see albedo in Chapter 2). Other losses are due to **scattering** and **absorption** by clouds, dust and gas molecules such as water vapour and ozone in the atmosphere.

Energy outputs

Compared to the sun, the Earth is a cool body that emits long-wave (or infrared) radiation (Figure 1.2). Only 5% of this **terrestrial radiation** escapes to space. The rest is absorbed by carbon dioxide, methane, water vapour and other greenhouse gases in the atmosphere. Most of this heat is trapped in the atmosphere and is re-radiated to the Earth's surface.

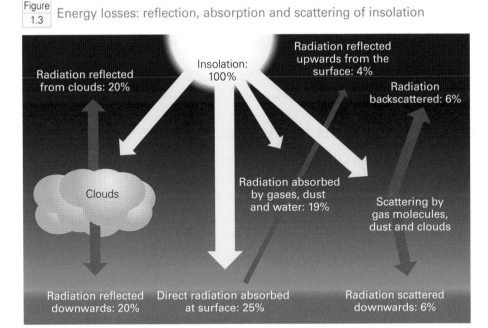

Figure 1.3 Energy losses: reflection, absorption and scattering of insolation

Over a year, and for the Earth as a whole, outputs of terrestrial radiation equal inputs of solar radiation. As a result, the global energy system maintains long-term balance and stability.

Energy transfers

Insolation absorbed by the Earth's surface is converted to heat energy and raises the surface temperature. Heat is then transferred from the Earth's surface to the atmosphere by three processes: conduction, convection and radiation.

- **Conduction** is the transfer of heat through a substance such as soil, by the collision of rapidly moving molecules. During the day, heat from insolation penetrates only a few centimetres into the soil. At night, this heat transfer is reversed. Thus soil has a limited heat capacity, quickly losing its accumulated daytime warmth by long-wave radiation at night.
- **Convection** describes the movement of liquids or gases containing heat brought about by changes in temperature, which affect density and create convection currents. On sunny days, heat is transferred from the ground surface to the atmosphere by convection. Air in contact with the warm ground is heated, becomes less dense than its surroundings, and rises as a column of warm air (a **thermal**) through the atmosphere.
- **Radiation** is the transfer of heat energy by electromagnetic waves emitted by all objects whose temperature is above absolute zero (−273 °C).

Energy can also be transferred horizontally as large bodies of warm air. In the British Isles, the horizontal transfer of sensible heat (i.e. heat that can be sensed and results in temperature change) from the subtropics often brings remarkably mild weather, and temperatures well above average. Heat energy is also transferred as latent heat, which is released on condensation and the formation of clouds, fog and dew (see Chapter 2).

Regional variations in the energy budget

While, at the global scale, the energy budget is in equilibrium, at the regional scale this balance disappears. Between the equator and latitude 40°, inputs of solar radiation exceed outputs of terrestrial radiation, creating a positive annual surplus of heat energy. In middle and high latitudes, the position is reversed: here annual energy losses exceed gains, giving rise to an energy budget deficit (Figure 1.4).

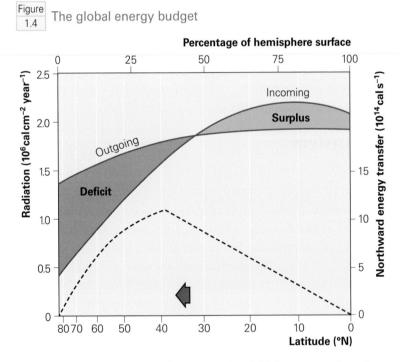

Figure 1.4 The global energy budget

These energy imbalances cannot be maintained: if they were, then the topics and subtropics would get warmer every year, while middle and high latitudes would get colder. The fact that climate stability is maintained is due to the redistribution of global heat energy. Surplus heat energy in low latitudes is transferred polewards by planetary winds and warm surface ocean currents, making good the energy deficit in high latitudes. Both the **general circulation** of the atmosphere (see below) and the **thermohaline circulation** of the oceans (Figure 1.5) are driven by regional differences in the energy budget.

Figure
1.5 Global thermohaline circulation

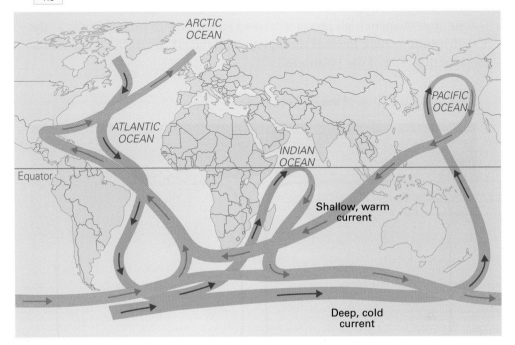

The general circulation of the atmosphere

Geographical imbalances in the energy budget, with an energy surplus in low latitudes and a deficit in middle and high latitudes, drive the atmosphere's general circulation.

The tropics

Between the equator and the subtropics the general circulation is dominated by the **Hadley cells** — two huge convective cells, one in each hemisphere (Figure 1.6). Around the equator, extreme instability (see Chapter 3) causes warm air to rise at the **inter-tropical convergence zone** (ITCZ). On reaching the level of the **tropopause** (see Fig. 1.1), this air diverges and flows towards the poles. As it does so, it cools and its density increases until, at around latitudes 20–30°, it slowly sinks towards the surface. Subsidence compresses and warms the air, preventing cloud formation. The result is clear skies, intense heating at the surface during the summer months and permanently dry weather. Thus subsiding air on the poleward limb of the Hadley cells explains the location of the world's great tropical deserts and the subtropical 'high' pressure belt. This zone of permanent high pressure drives a return flow of surface winds — the **trade winds** — back towards the equator and the ITCZ, which completes the convective cycle of the Hadley cells.

Figure 1.6 The circulation of the Hadley cells

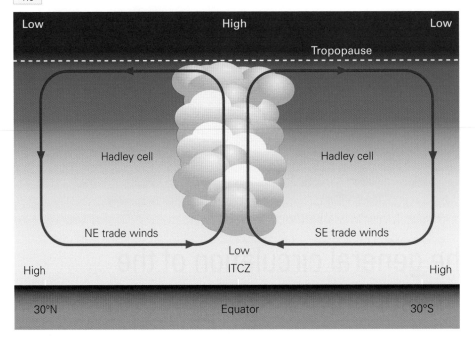

Middle latitudes

The general circulation in middle latitudes, known as the **Ferrel cell**, is more complex. The weather is dominated by a westerly airflow in which migrating **depressions** (areas of low pressure) and **anticyclones** (areas of high pressure) are embedded. This westerly flow is linked to a narrow, fast-moving belt of air known as the **polar front jet stream**, which encircles the northern and southern hemisphere in a series of waves (Figure 1.7). The jet stream steers the air masses, depressions and anticyclones responsible for the weather in middle latitudes.

Figure 1.7 The polar front jet stream and Rossby waves

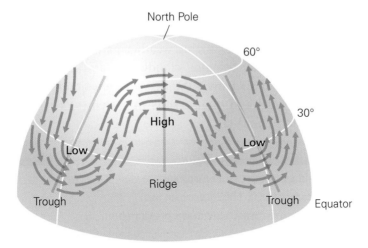

The polar front jet stream

Cold polar air and warm tropical air meet between latitudes 40° and 60°, where they create a sharp boundary. This is known as the **polar front**. Temperature contrasts along the front are abrupt and produce large pressure differences 8–10 km above the Earth's surface. Pressure at this level is high in the warm air to the south and low in the cold air to the north. The resulting pressure gradient generates strong winds moving at speeds of up to 300 km h^{-1} in the upper troposphere (roughly at the height that jet airliners fly).

In addition to the pressure gradient force, a second force — the **Coriolis force** (see Chapter 4) — influences the jet stream. The Coriolis force, caused by the Earth's axial rotation from west to east, deflects the wind to the right in the northern hemisphere, and to the left in the southern hemisphere. It balances the pressure gradient force so that the jet stream follows a roughly **zonal** path (i.e. along lines of latitude) from west to east.

In the northern hemisphere, the polar front jet stream encircles middle and high latitudes in four to six large meandering waves known as **Rossby waves** (Figure 1.7). The waves, separated by ridges and troughs, vary in wavelength and amplitude week by week as they move from west to east. The **ridges** are associated with warm air pushing polewards and are areas of high pressure; the **troughs** are areas of cold air and low pressure pushing south.

The jet stream steers air masses; generates travelling depressions and anti-cyclones; and controls day-to-day changes in temperature, precipitation and wind in middle latitudes (for more detail see Chapter 7). The wave-like pattern of the polar front jet stream (i.e. the Rossby waves) in the northern hemisphere is in part a response to the north–south relief barrier of the Rocky Mountains in North America.

The configuration of the Rossby waves (i.e. wavelength and amplitude) exerts a strong influence on changing weather patterns. With fewer waves, the airflow is more zonal, bringing cloudy, wet and cool conditions (see Chapter 9). With five or six waves, the flow becomes more **meridional** (i.e. along lines of longitude) and often results in extremes of temperature and drought (see Chapters 7 and 11).

Activity 1

Find jet stream and surface pressure maps at:

www.metcheck.com/V40/UK/FREE/jetstream.asp

www.metoffice.gov.uk/weather/uk/surface_pressure.html

For a period of 3 or 4 days, describe the changing position of the jet stream and its effect on (a) surface pressure, and (b) weather.

The North Atlantic Oscillation (NAO)

The **North Atlantic Oscillation** (NAO) describes the large-scale pattern of weather variability in the North Atlantic region. It is most important in winter and is associated with the north-to-south shifts in the tracks of depressions. With a deeper-than-normal low over Iceland and high pressure over the Azores, a strong westerly flow develops in response to the steep pressure gradient. In winter, weather conditions are warmer and wetter than average across western Europe as storm tracks move further south. In this

| Figure 1.8 | The North Atlantic Oscillation: 17 September 2009–14 January 2010 |

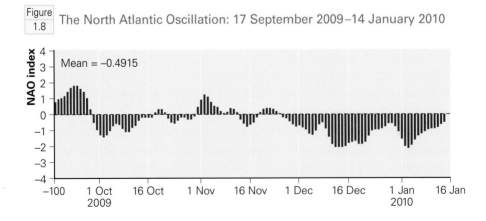

phase, the NAO has a **positive index** (Figure 1.8). A **negative index** occurs when the Azores 'high' is weaker than normal and pressure is relatively high in the North Atlantic around Iceland. This situation results in a breakdown in the westerly flow; blocking anticyclones (see Chapters 7 and 11); a greater frequency of northerly and easterly winds; and colder and drier conditions than normal.

High latitudes

The atmospheric circulation in high latitudes is cellular and similar in structure to the circulation in the tropics and subtropics. The **polar cell** is driven by radiative cooling, with cold air sinking near the poles and rising near latitude 60°. Cold dense air at the poles creates an area of permanent high pressure, producing an outward flow of surface easterly winds.

Activity 2

(a) Log on to: **www.cpc.noaa.gov/products/precip/CWlink/pna/nao_index.html**
Describe the fluctuations of the NAO over the past 6 months.

(b) Go to: **www.metoffice.gov.uk/climate/uk/2009/**
Explain how fluctuations in the NAO over the past 6 months may have influenced mean monthly temperatures and precipitation in the UK.

(c) Log on to: **www.cpc.noaa.gov/products/precip/CWlink/pna/nao.shtml**
Describe the forecast NAO for the next week and suggest how this is likely to influence the weather.

2 Frost, fog and cloud

Water vapour, although present in relatively small amounts in the atmosphere, has a huge influence on weather and climate. Without water vapour there would be no clouds and no precipitation. Temperatures would also be much lower because water vapour is an important greenhouse gas, and a highly effective absorber of long-wave radiation from the Earth. Most water vapour is concentrated near the Earth's surface, where it comprises up to 4% of the atmosphere by volume. However, in arid and semi-arid environments, the amounts of water vapour are much lower.

At temperatures normally found in the troposphere, water exists as a solid, a liquid and a gas. Indeed, individual clouds may contain ice particles, water droplets and water vapour at the same time.

Phase changes and latent heat

Phase changes are the processes responsible for the change of water between its different states (liquid, solid and gas) in the Earth–atmosphere system (Figure 2.1).

Latent heat is the heat energy needed to bring about a change of state from solid to liquid and from liquid to gas. Large inputs of energy are needed to break the molecular bonds of water in **evaporation** and **sublimation**. However, this energy input does not result in any rise in temperature of the water. Eventually the energy is released as latent heat in **condensation**, when water vapour becomes liquid water, and in **deposition** when vapour changes to ice.

Condensation and evaporation are the two most important phase changes that affect weather and climate.

- **Condensation** occurs when air is cooled to its dew-point temperature. Three circumstances promote cooling and condensation: (1) contact with a cold object such as the Earth's surface; (2) mixing of warmer air with cooler air; (3) dynamic expansion when air rises through the atmosphere. When condensation takes place, the subsequent release of latent heat warms the surrounding atmosphere.
- **Evaporation** is the phase change from liquid to vapour. It occurs as a result of either solar heating or wind movement and ceases when air becomes

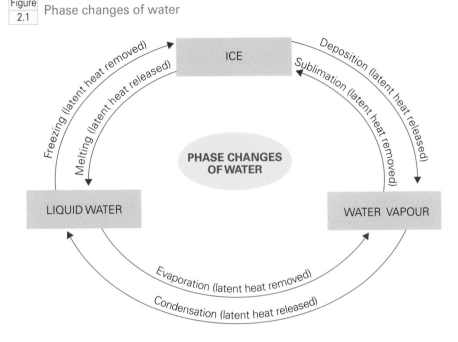

Figure
2.1 Phase changes of water

saturated. Because the evaporation process requires energy, it removes heat from a surface. This latent heat is later released on condensation.

Atmospheric humidity

Humidity describes the mass of water vapour in a given volume of air. The amount of water vapour in the air is temperature-dependent: warm air can hold more vapour than cold air (Table 2.1).

There are two common measures of humidity. **Absolute humidity** is the amount of water vapour in the air measured in grams per cubic metre ($g\,m^{-3}$). **Relative humidity** is the ratio between the amount of water vapour per cubic metre of air compared to the amount of water vapour the air can hold at saturation. It is usually

Table 2.1 The effect of temperature on the maximum amount of moisture in a cubic metre of air

Temperature (°C)	Amount of water ($g\,m^{-3}$) at saturation
–5	3.41
0	4.85
5	6.8
10	9.4
15	12.83
25	23.05

expressed as a percentage. Thus at 100% relative humidity, air is **saturated** and condensation should occur. Relative humidity varies from 100% (saturation) in fog or cloud to less than 10% in hot deserts. The critical temperature when saturation occurs is known as the **dew-point temperature**. In circumstances where the air is exceptionally pure, the absence of tiny particles (dust, sea salt) or condensation nuclei may delay condensation. The air is then said to be **supersaturated**.

- If the temperature is 10 °C and a cubic metre of air contains 5.64 grams of moisture, the relative humidity of the air will be (5.64 ÷ 9.4) × 100 = 60% (Table 2.1).

- The point of saturation (or dew point) is controlled by temperature. Cold air when saturated contains only small amounts of moisture. For example, at −5 °C a cubic metre of air can hold a maximum of 3.41 grams of moisture. However, at 25 °C air can hold a maximum of 23.05 grams.

- Dew point, as we have seen, is the critical temperature when air becomes saturated and condensation occurs. Suppose the air contains 6.8 grams of moisture per cubic metre at 10 °C. Its relative humidity would be (6.8 ÷ 9.4) × 100 = 72.3%. If the air were cooled to 5 °C, its humidity would increase to 100% ((6.8 ÷ 6.8) × 100). In other words, at 5 °C the air becomes saturated. Therefore 5 °C is the dew-point temperature of the air.

Activity 1

Study Figure 2.2.

(a) What is the maximum amount of water air can hold at: 10°C, 20°C, 30°C?

(b) If a parcel of air at 40°C holds 40g of moisture, what is its relative humidity?

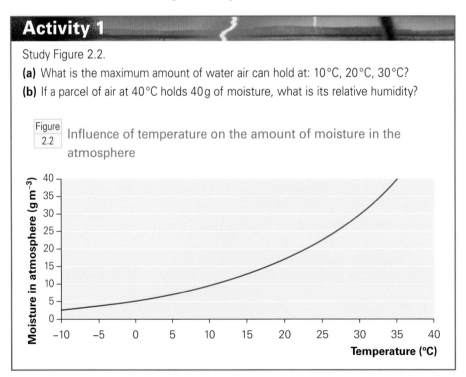

Figure 2.2 Influence of temperature on the amount of moisture in the atmosphere

Atmospheric moisture near the surface

When air in contact with the Earth's surface is cooled to its dew point it gives rise to a number of distinctive and closely related weather phenomena. They include dew, frost, rime, mist and fog.

Dew

Dew is water formed by condensation and deposited onto the ground surface, vegetation and other objects. It forms when long-wave radiation from the Earth's surface chills the overlying air to its dew point and causes condensation (Figure 2.3). The amount of dew deposited depends on the absolute humidity of the air, its temperature and wind speed. Ideal conditions for dew formation are:

- clear skies to maximise radiative cooling
- air close to saturation
- a light breeze

Strong winds prevent the formation of dew because the air does not remain in contact with the cold ground surface for long enough to reach its dew-point temperature. Dew most often forms at night and on exposed plant surfaces, insulated from the heat, which is conducted upwards through the soil.

Figure 2.3 Conditions favouring condensation and dew formation

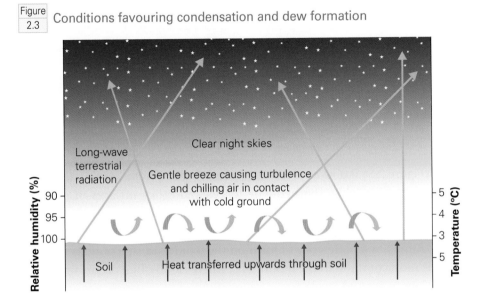

Frost

The term 'frost' is ambiguous, as it refers to at least three different weather phenomena. An **air frost** occurs when the air temperature above the ground falls to or below freezing (0 °C). If the ground temperature falls to or below freezing, it is known as a **ground** (or **grass**) **frost**. Both air and ground frosts are usually caused by radiative cooling of the ground at night. **Hoarfrost** (Figure 2.4) is the white crystalline deposit that forms on vegetation and other surfaces when ground temperatures fall to or below freezing. It consists of tiny ice crystals and should not be confused with frozen dew. Also, unlike dew, hoarfrost is formed by deposition (the phase change from vapour to solid) and not by condensation. This explains its crystalline form. Frozen dew or silver frost occurs when dew initially forms and temperatures later drop below freezing. This situation commonly occurs at night in winter when overcast conditions (which keep temperatures above freezing) give way to clear skies.

Figure 2.4 Hoarfrost

Michael Raw

Rime

Rime (Figure 2.5) is a layer of ice that forms on plant stems, leaves, telephone wires, electricity cables, barbed-wire fences and other surfaces. It is caused by freezing fog. When the tiny droplets of fog water collide with an object at sub-zero temperatures, they freeze on impact and gradually build up layers of ice. Rime has a preference to form on the windward side of objects. In the UK it is most common in the mountains, where cloud often occurs in freezing conditions at ground level.

Figure
2.5
Rime, due to prolonged sub-zero temperatures and hill fog

Michael Raw

Fog

Fog is cloud, comprising water droplets or ice particles or both, which extends to ground level. It restricts visibility to less than 1 km. Thick fog restricts visibility to less than 100 m and is a serious hazard to road traffic and aviation. **Mist** is similar to fog, except that its density is less, and visibility is not so restricted. There are several types of fog: radiation fog, hill fog, inversion (or valley) fog, advection fog and steam fog.

Radiation fog

Radiation fog forms over the land, especially at night and in winter (Figure 2.6). The conditions favouring its formation are similar to those for dew: clear

Figure
2.6
Early morning radiation fog at Carmona, Andalucia

Michael Raw

skies to promote radiative cooling; moist air close to saturation; and a light wind (Figure 2.7). A light wind is needed to spread the cooling some distance above the ground. Like dew, radiation fog does not form in windy conditions. Once fog droplets have formed, further cooling takes place

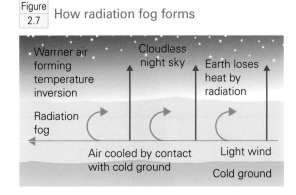

Figure 2.7 How radiation fog forms

by long-wave radiation from the droplets themselves.

Fog clears through evaporation caused either by solar heating or by an increase in wind speed. However, in winter, the sun's rays are often too weak to disperse radiation fog, which may persist all day. Radiation fog occurs in all seasons but is most common in winter with long hours of darkness, low temperatures and air close to saturation.

Ground fog is a type of radiation fog (Figure 2.8). However, unlike radiation fog, it is patchy and often no more than a few metres deep. It tends to form in topographic hollows and above areas of wet ground. Ground fog often develops briefly after sunset in winter, and in the early hours of the morning in summer. It occupies hollows where cold, dense air accumulates, and poorly drained areas where humidity is high.

Figure 2.8 Ground fog forming at sunset: mid-winter in Thetford Forest

Hill fog

In the British Isles, upland areas above 600 m may be covered in cloud for much of the year. To an observer on the ground, this cloud appears the same as fog and is given the name **hill fog** (Figure 2.9). Hill fog differs from radiation fog in the cooling process responsible for its formation. It develops when an air mass meets an upland area and is forced to rise mechanically. This **orographic** effect cools the air as it ascends and expands, due to the decrease in pressure with height — a process known as **adiabatic expansion**. Once the temperature of the air mass reaches dew point, condensation occurs and cloud or fog develops.

Figure 2.9	Hill fog above Hayeswater, Cumbria

Michael Raw

Inversion or valley fog

Normally temperatures decrease with height in the troposphere, a condition known as a **temperature lapse**. However, on some occasions, temperatures actually increase with height, creating what is known as an inversion. Inversions often develop at night when radiative cooling of the Earth's surface chills the overlying air, making it colder than the air above.

Figure 2.10 shows how, in some circumstances, local relief creates

Figure 2.10	The formation of inversion fog

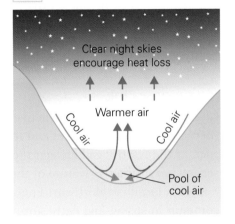

Clear night skies encourage heat loss

Warmer air

Cool air

Cool air

Pool of cool air

temperature inversions. Around sunset, air on the higher valley slopes loses heat more rapidly than air at the same height above the valley, and in the valley floor. Because cold air is denser than warm air, the cold air at higher levels slides down the valley slopes under gravity. Eventually it fills the valley bottom and lower slopes. Lighter, warmer air is then displaced above it, forming a lid on top of the cold air. The result is an inversion, where temperatures increase with height. If the cold air at the valley bottom is chilled to its dew point, radiation fog fills the lower valley (Figure 2.11).

Figure 2.11	Valley fog, Easdale

Michael Raw

In winter, deep valleys can experience extreme low temperatures. Hollows on the valley floor trap the cold air and give rise to **frost pockets**. It is no coincidence that the lowest temperatures ever recorded in the UK (–27.2 °C) are in deep glens in the Scottish Highlands. Frost can be a major hazard to farmers, damaging blossom and killing young plants. For this reason, orchards and vineyards are sited away from valley bottoms, on higher slopes where frosts are less frequent.

Advection or sea fog

Coastal areas often have distinctive local climates. This is due to the different thermal properties of the sea and the land. Along some stretches of coastline, such as the North Sea between the Humber and Tay estuaries, **advection** or **sea fog** is a distinctive feature of the local climate.

Known locally in northeast England as the 'sea fret', advection fog is most common in spring and early summer. At this time the differences between sea-surface temperatures and air temperatures are at their greatest. Even by late May, surface temperatures in the North Sea barely reach double figures, whereas air temperatures often exceed 20 °C. These differences favour the formation of advection fog (Figure 2.12).

| Figure 2.12 | Advection fog or sea fret at Burnmouth in late May |

Michael Raw

Along the North Sea coast, advection fog forms when an easterly wind transfers warm air from Scandinavia. As the warm air contacts the cold sea surface, three things happen: the air is chilled; turbulence caused by friction between the air mass and the sea surface spreads the cooling through

| Figure 2.13 | Advection fog |

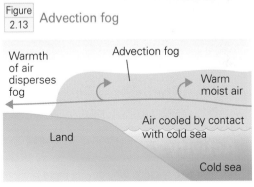

several hundred metres of the atmosphere; and evaporation over the sea increases the air's humidity (Figure 2.13).

Eventually, the air is cooled to its dew point, leading to condensation and the formation of fog over the sea and the coast. As the fog moves onshore, the warmer land causes it to evaporate or lift to form low stratus cloud. Further inland, skies will be clear.

Advection fog makes the climate of the coast of northeast England markedly less sunny than the northwest coast at similar latitudes. It can also lead to unusually low temperatures in late spring and early summer. For example, with a cover of advection fog in early June, temperatures may struggle to reach 10 °C in Newcastle-upon-Tyne or Scarborough, while the rest of the country basks in unbroken sunshine and temperatures into the mid-20s.

Steam fog

Steam fog is a shallow layer of fog that forms over rivers and lakes, especially in autumn (Figure 2.14). It develops when the water is warmer than the overlying air. This often happens when a temperature inversion forms in a valley overnight. As water is evaporated from the river or lake, it is immediately chilled by contact with the cold air above. When cooling is sufficient to trigger condensation, steam fog forms.

| Figure 2.14 | Steam fog on the Connecticut River, Massachusetts |

Michael Raw

Activity 2

(a) Give two reasons why dew is more likely to form in winter than in summer.

(b) Explain why dew deposits are small in still-air conditions.

(c) Explain why ground frost is more common than air frost.

(d) Why does radiation fog never form over lakes, seas and oceans?

(e) Why are the seas and oceans around the British Isles warmer than the land in winter, but cooler in summer?

(f) Investigate the contrasts in sea-surface temperatures and land temperatures in the British Isles. Sea-surface temperatures for the North Sea can be obtained from: **www.bsh.de/aktdat/mk/nordsee/actual.gif**. Archive temperatures for individual stations are available at: **www.weatheronline.co.uk**

Atmospheric moisture above the surface

Clouds

Clouds are visible aggregates of minute particles of water or ice, or both, that float in the free air. The earliest classification of clouds was based on their shape or appearance, and dates from the early nineteenth century. It is still used today. This classification recognises three main cloud types (Figure 2.15):

- **Cumulus** (Cu) — cauliflower-like, with flat bases and considerable vertical development (Figure 2.15a)
- **Cirrus** (Ci) — delicate, high-altitude clouds with a fibrous or feathery appearance (Figure 2.15b)
- **Stratus** (St) — layer clouds, at low altitude and with no great depth (Figure 2.15c)

Figure 2.15 Cloud types:
(a) cumulus
(b) cirrus
(c) stratus

Michael Raw

(a)

(b)

(c)

Table 2.2 shows a more detailed classification, with cloud types identified by both appearance and altitude.

Table 2.2	Classification of cloud types according to altitude
Low clouds < 2500 m	Stratus (St), Strato-cumulus (Sc), Cumulus (Cu), Fracto-stratus (Fs), Fracto-cumulus (Fc)
Middle clouds 2500–6000 m	Alto-cumulus (Ac), Alto-stratus (As)
High clouds > 6000 m	Cirrus (Ci), Cirro-stratus (Cs), Cirro-cumulus (Cc)
Clouds with vertical development	Nimbo-stratus (Ns), Cumulo-nimbus (Cb)
Latin terms: stratus = layer; cumulus = heap; fractus = broken; nimbus = raincloud; altus = high; cirrus = fibre	

Activity 3

Check out the Cloud Appreciation Society's website and gallery at:
www.cloudappreciationsociety.org/gallery. Familiarise yourself with the appearance of the cloud types listed in Table 2.2.

Cloud formation

Clouds form when water vapour is chilled to its dew point and condensation (or deposition) occurs. Cooling takes place when:
- parcels of warm air rise freely through the atmosphere (in convection currents) and cool by expansion due to pressure change (adiabatic expansion)
- an air mass moves horizontally across a relatively cooler surface (advection)
- an air mass rises as it crosses a mountain barrier or turbulence causes its forced ascent (adiabatic expansion)
- a relatively warm air mass mixes with a cooler one

Stability and instability

The key to understanding the free ascent of air in the atmosphere is the concept of **stability** and **instability**. When conditions are unstable, an air parcel displaced from its initial position, by either heating or mechanical uplift, rises freely through the atmosphere. Ascent occurs because the displaced air is warmer, and therefore less dense, than its surroundings. Unstable conditions lead to the development of **cumuliform** clouds, often accompanied by precipitation, usually in the form of showers. Stable conditions are the exact opposite. When an air parcel is displaced, it returns to its original level because it remains cooler, and therefore denser, than the surrounding air.

Clouds formed in unstable conditions

Cumuliform clouds develop when the atmosphere is unstable. Convection is triggered by differences in the colour and texture of the ground surface, which affect rates of heat absorption. Thus dark surfaces such as soil and forests absorb more heat and therefore become warmer than lighter coloured surfaces such as ice and sand. We refer to this condition as the **albedo** or reflectivity of a surface. Fresh snow reflects up to 90% of incident solar radiation and has the highest albedo of any natural surface (see Table 2.3).

Table 2.3 Albedos for short-wave solar radiation

Surface	Percentage reflected	Surface	Percentage reflected
Water (angles > 40°)	2–4	Grass	10–20
Water (angles < 40°)	6–80	Coniferous forest	5–15
Fresh snow	75–90	Crops	15–25
Dry sand	35–45	Dark, wet soil	5–15

If a surface has a low albedo, as with a ploughed field, the ground will heat up rapidly. This heat will transfer to the overlying air until bubbles of warm air begin to break away from the surface and rise as a convection current or thermal. As the warm air rises, it expands adiabatically (due to lower pressure and a loss of energy) and cools. Eventually, when it reaches the dew-point level in the atmosphere, it condenses and forms cloud (Figure 2.16).

Figure 2.16 Instability

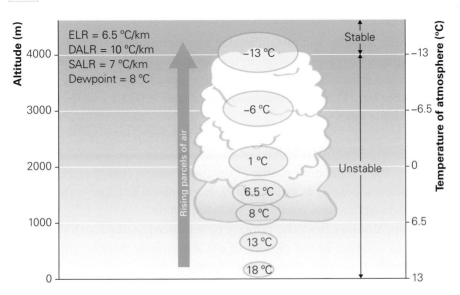

Clouds formed in stable conditions

Clouds also form in stable conditions. When relatively warm air moves across a cooler surface (e.g. the ocean) and its lowest layers are chilled to dew point, extensive layer or **stratiform** clouds develop. This is the process of advection that also gives rise to advection fog or sea fog. The difference is that wind speeds near the surface are too high to permit prolonged contact that would otherwise chill the air to its dew point. At higher levels, temperatures are low enough to reach dew point, resulting in condensation and the formation of stratus cloud.

Clouds formed in hills and mountains

Clouds may form in hills and mountains regardless of the stability or instability of the atmosphere. This is because air is mechanically lifted when it encounters major relief features. In stable conditions, clouds form above the condensation level on **windward** slopes as air ascends a hill or mountain barrier, and clouds evaporate as air descends and warms on the **leeward** slopes. Over the summits, clouds formed in such stable conditions will have limited depth. The result is a cloud that appears to be more or less fixed in position over hills and mountains and may linger all day.

However, it is not uncommon for air that is initially stable to become unstable at altitude. This is known as **conditional instability**. In this situation, the atmosphere is only unstable above a certain height. Depending on the depth of the unstable layer, clouds formed in these circumstances may be several kilometres thick.

Lapse rates and atmospheric stability and instability

Atmospheric stability and instability can be determined by examining **lapse rates**. A temperature lapse is a fall in temperature that occurs with increasing height in the atmosphere. There are three types of lapse rate: the **environmental lapse rate** (ELR); the **dry adiabatic lapse rate** (DALR); and the **saturated adiabatic lapse rate** (SALR).

Environmental lapse rate (ELR)

The ELR is the temperature profile of the lower atmosphere (i.e. its temperature at different heights at a given time). It averages $6.5\ °C\,km^{-1}$. The reasons why the atmosphere gets cooler with height include:

- increasing distance from the primary heat source (i.e. the Earth's surface)
- the rapid decrease in the density of the atmosphere with height (making heat transfer from the ground less efficient)

- the lower concentration of water vapour (a greenhouse gas) and heat-absorbing dust particles at higher altitudes

Dry adiabatic lapse rate (DALR)

The DALR is the rate at which a parcel of dry air (i.e. less than 100% humidity) cools with altitude. Cooling is by dynamic expansion (i.e. there is no energy exchange with the surrounding atmosphere) and is approximately $10\,°C\,km^{-1}$. This cooling caused by expansion is termed adiabatic.

Saturated adiabatic lapse rate (SALR)

Like the DALR, the SALR also relates to parcels of rising air. It is defined as the rate at which a parcel of saturated air cools (i.e. one in which condensation is occurring) as it rises through the atmosphere. Cooling is again due to dynamic expansion but at $7\,°C\,km^{-1}$ the SALR is lower than the DALR. The reason for this is that condensation releases latent heat, reducing the average rate of temperature fall.

Figure 2.17 Atmospheric stability and instability: (a) absolute instability; (b) absolute stability; (c) conditional instability

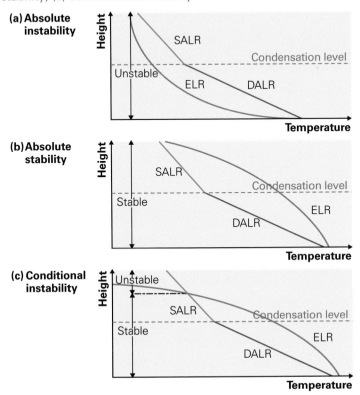

Activity 4

Study the lapse rate diagrams in Figure 2.17.

(a) What is meant by the terms: environmental lapse rate, dry adiabatic lapse rate, and saturated adiabatic lapse rate?

(b) Why is the saturated adiabatic lapse rate less than the dry adiabatic lapse rate?

(c) Give a brief explanation of atmospheric stability/instability shown in each of the three diagrams in Figure 2.17.

(d) Sketch the diagrams in Figure 2.17 and show the probable extent of cloud.

3 Precipitation

Definition

Precipitation occurs when particles of liquid water or ice formed within a cloud fall towards the ground. In some circumstances, precipitation does not reach the ground. It can, for example, evaporate on the way down especially if the air through which it falls is warm and dry.

Table 3.1 Types of precipitation

Type	Description
Rain	Water droplets with a diameter > 0.5 mm
Drizzle	Fine droplets with a diameter < 0.5 mm and very close to one another
Freezing rain	Rain (or drizzle) that freezes on impact with the ground
Snowflakes	Loose aggregates of ice crystals, most of which are branched
Sleet	Partly melted snowflakes or rain and snow falling together
Snow pellets (soft hail or graupel)	White, opaque grains of ice, spherical or sometimes conical, with a diameter about 0.2–0.5 mm
Snow grains (granular snow)	Very small, white opaque grains of ice generally < 1 mm in diameter
Ice pellets	Transparent or translucent spheroidal particles of ice
Hail	Small balls or pieces of ice with diameters normally in the range 5–50 mm but sometimes more
Ice prisms	Unbranched ice crystals in the form of needles, columns and plates

Formation of rain

Tiny water droplets that form clouds are pulled by gravity towards the Earth's surface. However, they fall so slowly (terminal velocity $0.01\,\text{m s}^{-1}$) that they are kept aloft by the vertical currents caused by convection and turbulence.

Rain droplets are on average 200–600 times larger in diameter than cloud droplets. The terminal velocity of a 4 mm raindrop is around $9\,\text{m sec}^{-1}$, which is sufficient for it to fall out of clouds as precipitation. The key question is: how do such tiny cloud droplets become large enough to form rain? There are two theories: the collision theory; and the Bergeron–Findeisen theory.

Collision theory

Some of the droplets are larger than others and consequently their fall speed is greater. These larger droplets overtake and collide with smaller ones, sweeping them up and becoming larger. As a result of this process, rain droplets can reach 0.2 mm in diameter in around 50 minutes. Eventually the water droplets become too heavy to remain in suspension and fall from the base of the cloud. Collision theory provides the main explanation for precipitation from clouds situated below the freezing level and is therefore most relevant in the tropics.

Bergeron–Findeisen theory

In middle and high latitudes, precipitation often falls from clouds above the freezing level. Such clouds consist of a mixture of tiny ice particles and **supercooled** water droplets that remain liquid, despite sub-zero temperatures. The co-existence of ice and water droplets is seen as crucial to the rainmaking process. Because vapour pressure is higher over supercooled water than ice, water vapour is evaporated from the water droplets and deposited on adjacent ice particles. Thus the ice particles grow at the expense of the water droplets until they reach a critical mass and fall from the cloud. If temperatures below the cloud base are above freezing, the ice particles melt as they descend and fall as rain. However, if sub-zero temperatures extend to (or close to) the ground, precipitation may fall as snow or sleet. Evidence of this is seen in upland regions where precipitation that falls as snow on higher ground often turns to rain at lower levels in the valleys (Figure 3.1).

| Figure 3.1 | Snowline on the Scafell range after heavy overnight snow |

Michael Raw

Other forms of precipitation

Only clouds with significant depth (i.e. 1000 m or more) will produce rain. However, **drizzle** often forms by collision in shallow stratus clouds less than 300 m deep. Other conditions which favour drizzle include: (1) the absence of any significant vertical motion which would otherwise keep the tiny droplets (0.2–0.5 mm diameter) in suspension; (2) high relative humidity between the cloud base and the surface to prevent the falling droplets from evaporating.

Snow is frozen precipitation resulting from ice crystal growth as explained by the Bergeron–Findeisen process. There are many types of snow, from small crystals to large flakes. Snow may reach the surface or melt below the freezing level and fall as rain or sleet. Snowflakes are made up of hundreds of snow crystals that have collided and stuck together in clusters. Most aggregation occurs at temperatures just below freezing; at lower temperatures individual snow crystals tend to remain separate.

Hail consists of small balls or pieces of ice that usually range in diameter from 5 mm to 50 mm. It develops above the freezing level in thick cumulonimbus clouds that often reach the tropopause. Within these clouds, powerful **updraughts** and **downdraughts** exist side by side (Figure 3.2, and see Chapters 7 and 8). Updraughts sweep ice particles to the top of the cloud where temperatures can reach –50 °C. As the particles circulate within the cloud, they pass through areas of supercooled water droplets

Figure
3.2 Hail formation

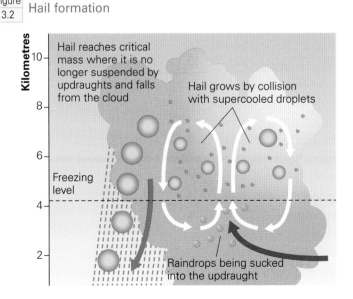

Kilometres

10 — Hail reaches critical mass where it is no longer suspended by updraughts and falls from the cloud

Hail grows by collision with supercooled droplets

8 —

6 —

Freezing level

4 —

2 —

Raindrops being sucked into the updraught

and become coated in glassy ice. This process may be repeated several times and each time the hail grows by accretion. In the tropics and continental interiors in mid-latitudes, updraughts are so strong that hailstones weighing up to 2 kg can form.

Intensity and duration of precipitation events

Intensity

Precipitation intensity is the amount of precipitation that falls in a given time period, usually in 1 hour or 1 day. In the UK, rainfall intensity rarely exceeds 25 mm an hour. Figure 3.3 shows a rainfall event of unusual intensity in the UK for the period 4–6 September 2008. Extreme rainfall intensities may exceed 25 mm a minute, and 250 mm an hour (Table 3.2). However, most high-intensity events are short-lived, lasting for no more than an hour.

Duration

The duration of any precipitation event depends on the persistence of the cloud from which it falls.

On the basis of duration, we group precipitation events into two types: general precipitation and showers.

- **General precipitation** is associated with frontal systems and extensive layer clouds such as strato-cumulus and nimbo-stratus. It starts and stops slowly,

Figure 3.3 Rainfall in the UK for 4–6 September 2008 (mm)

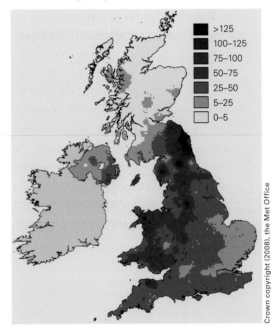

| >125 |
| 100–125 |
| 75–100 |
| 50–75 |
| 25–50 |
| 5–25 |
| 0–5 |

Crown copyright (2008), the Met Office

Table 3.2 Extreme rainfall intensities

Total rainfall (mm)	Time	Place
38	1 minute	Guadeloupe
401	1 hour	Shangdi, Inner Mongolia
1825	1 day	La Réunion
5003	1 week	La Réunion
12 767	1 month	Cherrapunji, Assam

often lasts for several hours with or without breaks, and is generally of low intensity.

- **Showers** are generated by isolated cumuliform clouds such as cumulonimbus. They usually start and stop suddenly, seldom last for more than an hour, and are typically high-intensity events.

Precipitation types

The processes responsible for cooling and condensation that ultimately result in precipitation are used to recognise three general precipitation types. They are convectional, frontal and orographic (or relief) precipitation.

Convectional precipitation

Convection occurs when an air mass is heated from below, becomes warmer and less dense than its surroundings, and rises freely through the atmosphere. The trigger for instability is most often differential heating of the ground by solar radiation. However, convection can also occur through advection, when a relatively cool air mass moves horizontally across a warmer surface. Convectional precipitation takes the form of showers from cumuliform clouds and is often of high intensity and accompanied by thunder and lightning. In mid-latitudes, convection precipitation is largely confined to the summer months. In the tropics, it is the main type of precipitation throughout the year.

Frontal precipitation

Frontal systems are boundaries between air masses of contrasting temperature and humidity. Active frontal systems in mid-latitude depressions generate large amounts of cloud and precipitation. In the warm sector of a depression, a tongue of warm air runs parallel to and ahead of the cold front. Near the centre of the depression it turns abruptly to the right and flows parallel to and rises above the warm front. This is known as the **warm air conveyor belt** (Figure 3.4). As

| Figure 3.4 | The warm air conveyor belt |

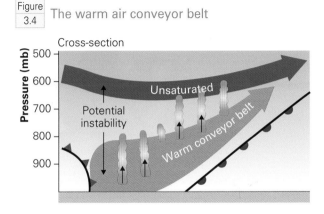

Cross-section

the air ascends, it cools adiabatically, filling the troposphere (5–6 km) with cloud and producing prolonged general precipitation.

Frontal precipitation is also found at the cold front in a depression, where colder air replaces warmer air. The cold dense air behind the cold front forces the warmer, lighter air aloft, producing thick cumuliform clouds. Precipitation is often more intense but of shorter duration than at the warm front. At both warm and cold fronts, **convection cells** (rising columns of warmer air) embedded in the warm sector may produce intensive bursts of precipitation.

Orographic precipitation

Mountains receive higher amounts of precipitation than adjacent lowlands (Figure 3.5), and a larger proportion of this precipitation falls as snow. Higher precipitation is explained by the physical obstruction of mountains to approaching air masses, forcing the air aloft. Mechanical uplift usually results in cloud formation and, where the cloud is thick enough, precipitation. Precipitation formed in this way is known as **relief** or **orographic precipitation** (Figure 3.6). This is exemplified in Figure 3.7 where precipitation associated with an active frontal system has been intensified by uplift over the Lake District and southern uplands of Scotland.

Air that may be stable at low altitude often becomes unstable at higher levels. In the British Isles it is common to find that stable air forced aloft by mountains becomes unstable at altitude and continues to rise freely. This situation

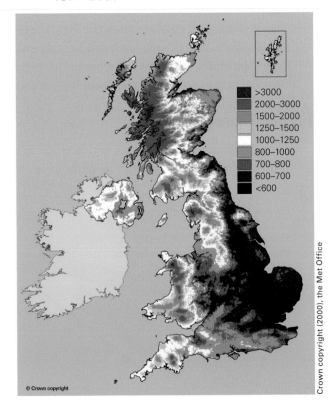

Figure 3.5 UK annual average rainfall (mm), 1971–2000

>3000
2000–3000
1500–2000
1250–1500
1000–1250
800–1000
700–800
600–700
<600

© Crown copyright

Crown copyright (2000), the Met Office

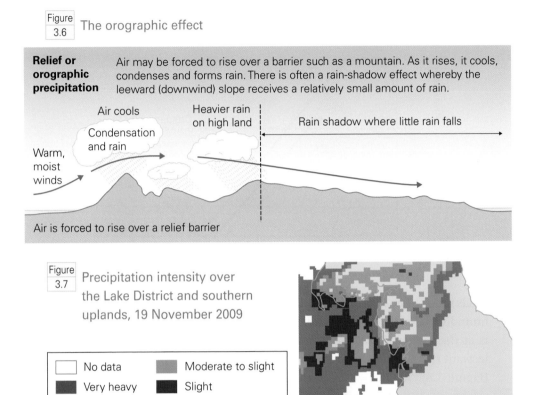

Figure 3.6 The orographic effect

Relief or orographic precipitation Air may be forced to rise over a barrier such as a mountain. As it rises, it cools, condenses and forms rain. There is often a rain-shadow effect whereby the leeward (downwind) slope receives a relatively small amount of rain.

Air cools

Condensation and rain

Warm, moist winds

Heavier rain on high land

Rain shadow where little rain falls

Air is forced to rise over a relief barrier

Figure 3.7 Precipitation intensity over the Lake District and southern uplands, 19 November 2009

No data

Very heavy

Heavy

Moderate

Moderate to slight

Slight

Very slight

of conditional instability (see Chapter 2) adds significantly to precipitation amounts and intensities in mountain and upland regions such as the Western Highlands, the Lake District and Snowdonia.

While the summits and windward slopes of mountains invariably experience above-average precipitation, the leeward slopes, facing downwind, are relatively dry and lie in a so-called **rain shadow**. There are two reasons for this rain-shadow effect:

- Large amounts of moisture are expended as precipitation and cloud on windward slopes and summits, and thus absolute humidity is lower on leeward slopes.
- Air descending leeward slopes is warmed dynamically by adiabatic compression, due to rising pressure. As a result, clouds begin to evaporate and the likelihood of precipitation is reduced.

The dynamic warming process involves another factor. Forced ascent of moist air results in cooling at the SALR (7 °C km^{-1}; see Chapter 2). As this rising air

Figure
3.8
Föhn effect (temperature–height)

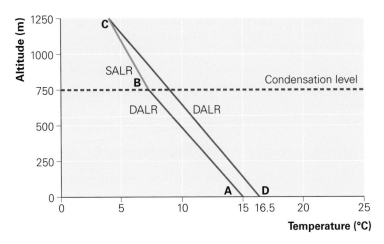

sheds much of its moisture over the summits and windward slopes, its relative humidity falls below 100%. Thus warming on descent of leeward slopes is at the higher DALR (10 °C km^{-1}). This raises the air temperature on the leeward slope above that on the windward slope at the corresponding altitude (Figure 3.8). Such flows of warm dry air on leeward mountain slopes create a **föhn effect** as well as a rain shadow. In the British Isles the föhn effect is most notable around the Moray Firth in Scotland when winds blow from the southwest across the Grampians. Far more dramatic is the chinook wind that blows from the Rockies to the prairies of Canada and the USA. In springtime the chinook (also called the 'snow eater') can raise temperatures of the plains by 20–30 °C in just a few hours.

Activity 1

(a) Describe the influence of relief on rainfall in the rainfall radar image (Figure 3.7) of the Lake District and southern uplands for 19 November 2009.

(b) Study the cross-section and the temperature–height diagram in Figure 3.8.

(c) Explain how (i) air rising between locations A and B cools; (ii) air descending from C to D warms.

(d) Explain the difference in temperature between locations A and D.

(e) Give two reasons why precipitation is lower on the leeward side than on the windward side of mountain or hill masses.

4 Pressure and winds

Atmospheric pressure and winds are closely connected. Spatial differences in pressure are caused by contrasts in (a) air temperature and air density; (b) rates at which air enters and leaves an air column. These pressure differences, known as **pressure gradients**, drive horizontal flows of air both at the Earth's surface and within the atmosphere.

Atmospheric pressure

The mass of gases that form the atmosphere exert a pressure that is measured in **millibars** (mb). Pressure decreases with height as the weight of the overlying air column decreases. However, because air is compressible, the rate of decrease is not linear. Thus about half the mass of the atmosphere is compressed into the lowest 5.5 km (Figure 4.1).

Figure 4.1 Changes in atmospheric pressure with altitude

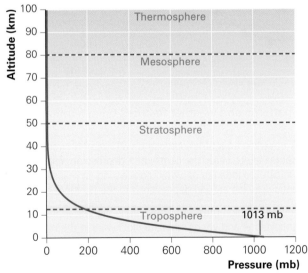

Because pressure is so sensitive to altitude, for the purposes of forecasting it is usually standardised to sea level. Average sea-level pressure is around 1013 mb. A deep low-pressure system or depression typically has a central pressure of 940–990 mb; a high-pressure cell or anticyclone normally ranges between 1020 and 1050 mb. Overall, horizontal spatial differences in pressure are relatively small.

Atmospheric pressure is mapped on weather charts using **isobars** or lines joining places of equal pressure. On synoptic charts used for weather forecasting, isobars are standardised to sea level and drawn at 4 mb intervals. We recognise a number of characteristic weather features from isobaric patterns on synoptic charts. They include depressions, anticyclones, ridges, troughs and cols (Figure 4.2).

Figure 4.2 Common pressure patterns on synoptic charts

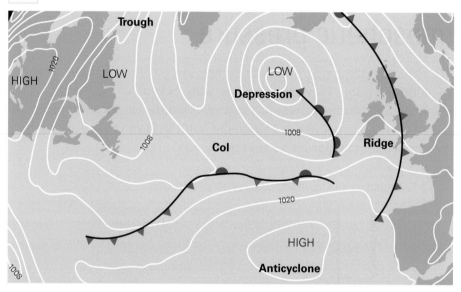

Table 4.1 Pressure patterns and weather features on synoptic charts

Depression	A travelling area of low pressure with roughly circular isobars. Pressure decreases towards the centre of a depression. Frontal systems indicate boundaries between contrasting air masses. Winds circulate anticlockwise around depressions in the northern hemisphere
Anticyclone	An area of high pressure. Pressure is highest at the centre of the anticyclone and winds circulate clockwise in the northern hemisphere. Most anticyclones comprise a single air mass and therefore lack frontal systems
Ridge	An outward extension of an area of high pressure
Trough	An outward extension of an area of low pressure
Col	An area of slack pressure gradient between two weather systems

Winds

Winds are horizontal movements of air that blow from high- to low-pressure areas. Large pressure differences over short distances create steep pressure gradients and strong winds. The **pressure gradient force** (PGF) is the master force that determines the direction and strength of the wind. It acts perpendicular to the isobars. Two other forces act on the wind: the Coriolis force and friction. The Coriolis force (CF), imparted by the rotation of the Earth on its axis, deflects the wind to the right of its otherwise expected path in the northern hemisphere and to the left in the southern hemisphere. It always acts at 90° to the direction of the wind (Figure 4.3). Because of the balance between the pressure gradient and Coriolis forces, winds flow parallel to isobars in the upper troposphere. This resultant balanced wind is known as the **geostrophic wind**. Near the Earth's surface, winds blow approximately parallel to the isobars.

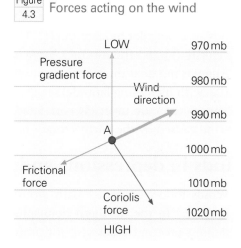

Figure 4.3 Forces acting on the wind

Friction between the wind and the Earth's surface acts in the opposite direction to the wind and slightly modifies wind direction near the surface. Because of the effect of friction at the surface, the wind there is no longer balanced. As a result it flows at a shallow angle to the isobars and is slightly **backed** (i.e. an anticlockwise change) compared to the geostrophic wind. The angle of this deflection depends on the roughness of the surface. Over the oceans, where friction is least, the wind crosses the isobars at about 10°. Over land, where there is greater resistance, the angle is around 30°.

Thus the combination of the pressure gradient force, the Coriolis force and friction determines the behaviour of the wind. It means that if you stand with your back to the wind in the northern hemisphere, low pressure is always on your left and high pressure on your right — a phenomenon known as Buys Ballot's law.

The Coriolis force

The Coriolis force is an apparent force caused by the rotation of the Earth on its axis. It deflects the wind to the right in the northern hemisphere and to the left in the southern hemisphere and always acts at 90° to the direction of the wind. The Coriolis force increases with latitude, being greatest at the poles and zero at the equator. Because the Earth is a rotating body, the wind possesses **angular momentum** (L). This is equal to the product of its **mass** (m), **velocity** (v) and the distance between the wind and the **axis of rotation** (r). Angular momentum is always conserved, so that any decrease in distance (r) (i.e. with increasing latitude) creates a corresponding increase in velocity (v). Thus v and r are inversely correlated. This accounts for the deflection of the wind caused by the Earth's rotation.

Winds in depressions and anticyclones

Winds follow a circular path around the isobars in depressions and anti-cyclones. In the northern hemisphere this circulation is anticlockwise for depressions and clockwise for anticyclones. The converse is found in the southern hemisphere.

Winds that follow a circular path are affected by another force — the **centripetal force**, which acts towards the centre of a depression or anticyclone. Thus a balanced wind, which is in equilibrium with the PGF, the CF and the centripetal force, flows parallel to the isobars along a curved path. This is the **gradient wind** (Figure 4.4). The gradient wind near the surface spirals inwards

Figure 4.4	Gradient wind

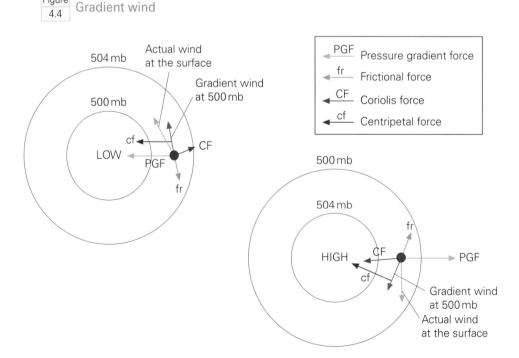

towards the centre of depressions (i.e. PGF > CF), while in anticyclones the gradient winds spirals outwards (CF > PGF). As a result, the gradient wind slows and is **subgeostrophic** in depressions, while in anticyclones it accelerates and is **supergeostrophic** (Figure 4.5).

Figure 4.5 Wind flow in depressions and anticyclones

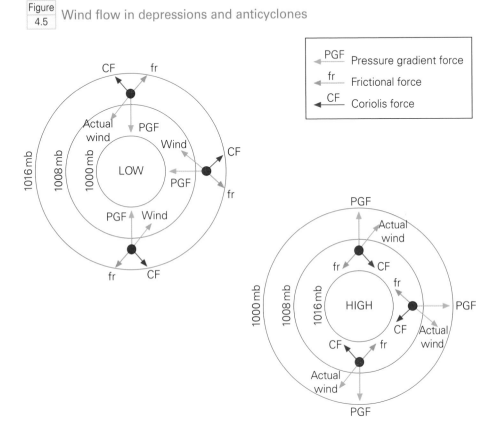

Wind direction and behaviour

Wind direction is the point on the compass from which the wind blows. Thus a westerly wind blows from west to east, and a southwesterly from southwest to northeast. **Prevailing winds** are the winds that blow most often at a particular place. In the British Isles, the southwesterlies, which blow around 30% of the time, are the prevailing winds. 'Backing' and 'veering' describe a change in wind direction. **Backing** is an anticlockwise change, and **veering** is a clockwise change. Winds often change direction at frontal zones in depressions: at the passage of both warm and cold fronts, winds veer or change in a clockwise direction (see Chapter 9).

Activity 1

(a) What evidence in Figure 3.5 in Chapter 3 suggests that the direction of the prevailing winds in the British Isles is southwest?

(b) Study the four Atlantic charts for 24 to 27 November (Figure 4.6). Complete questions (ii) and (ii) and enter your answers in Table 4.2.

   (i) Make photocopies of the charts and insert arrows to show the wind directions.

   (ii) Identify the wind direction and the likely origin of the wind on each chart.

   (iii) Describe the likely temperatures in the British Isles.

Figure 4.6	Atlantic synoptic charts, 24–27 November: (a) 24 November; (b) 25 November; (c) 26 November; (d) 27 November

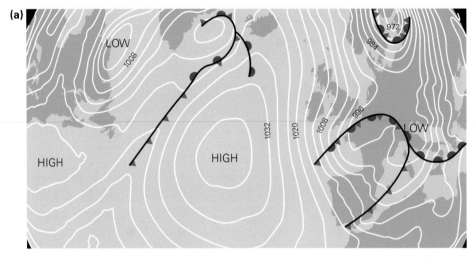

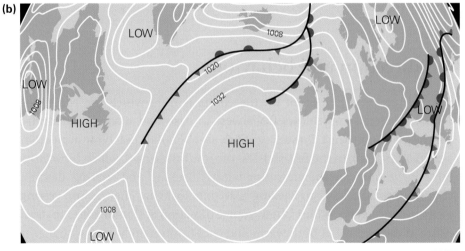

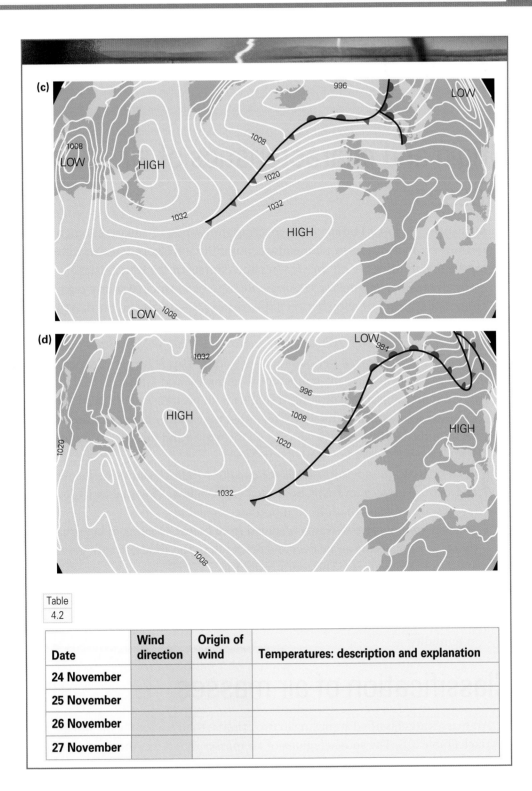

(c)

(d)

Table
4.2

Date	Wind direction	Origin of wind	Temperatures: description and explanation
24 November			
25 November			
26 November			
27 November			

5 Air masses

Origin and characteristics of air masses

Air masses are large bodies of air covering thousands of square kilometres. Defined by their uniform temperature, humidity and lapse rate, air masses exert a major influence on the weather and climate of the British Isles.

The air masses affecting the UK originate from two principal **source regions**. Tropical air masses develop between the Azores (30–40°N) and north Africa. Polar and arctic air masses form within the Arctic Circle over northern Canada, northern Eurasia and Svalbad. Both subtropical and polar source regions are quiet, settled areas of permanent anticyclone. This is no coincidence: air masses can only acquire the temperature, humidity and lapse rate characteristics of source regions by prolonged contact with ground and ocean surfaces.

Once an air mass leaves its source region, it undergoes changes in temperature, humidity and stability depending on the nature and direction of its **track**. These changes follow a few simple principles:

- Polar or arctic air moving towards the equator will track across warmer land and ocean surfaces and will be heated from below. This makes its lower layers warmer than air aloft, so it becomes unstable.
- Tropical air moving polewards is cooled from below. Cooling of layers near the surface makes the air heavier and denser than the air above and prevents any vertical movement. The result is stability.
- Air masses moving across an ocean or sea surface pick up moisture and become more humid.
- Air masses crossing continental surfaces undergo little or no modification in humidity.

Classification of air masses

Air masses are classified according to two criteria: their source region and their track (Table 5.1). The source regions of air masses that affect the weather and climate of the British Isles are tropical (T), polar (P) and arctic (A). Although both arctic and polar air masses are cold, they have different source regions. Arctic air masses, which are usually colder than polar air masses, originate over the Arctic Ocean close to the North Pole, whereas polar air masses form over northern Canada, Greenland and the northern and central Eurasian landmass. Once they have left their source region, air masses follow either a maritime (m) track over seas and oceans or a continental (c) track over land (Figure 5.1).

Table 5.1 Classification of air masses

Source region	Track	
	Maritime (m)	**Continental (c)**
Arctic (A)	Arctic maritime (Am)	Arctic continental (Ac)*
Polar (P)	Polar maritime (Pm)	Polar continental (Pc)
Tropical (T)	Tropical maritime (Tm)	Tropical continental (Tc)

*Important in North America but does not affect the British Isles

Frequency of air mass types

The character and variability of the UK's weather is strongly influenced by air masses, which invade northwest Europe from all directions (Figure 5.1). The influence of these air masses owes much to geography. First, the UK, situated on the extreme northwest periphery of the Eurasian landmass, is exposed both to oceanic and continental influences. Most air masses, particularly those from the west and north, have been modified by long oceanic tracks before reaching the UK. Even continental air masses moving west are modified by the short North Sea crossing. Second, the mid-latitude location of the UK means that it is never far from the polar front, and is a meteorological 'battleground' where cold polar air to the north meets warm tropical air to the south. During the winter months, the polar front and its associated jet stream lie for much of the time across northern Britain.

In the UK, the prevailing southwesterly winds mean that polar maritime (Pm)

Figure 5.1 Air masses affecting weather and climate in the British Isles

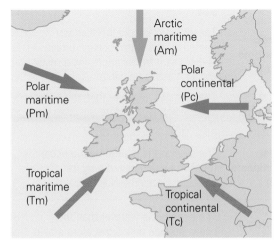

and tropical maritime (Tm) air mass types are most frequent. Continental influences in the form of polar continental (Pc; Figure 5.2) and tropical continental (Tc) are far less common (see Tables 5.2–5.4).

Table 5.2 Percentage frequency of air masses at Kew (London) and Stornoway (northwest Scotland)

	Kew	Stornoway
Arctic maritime (Am)	6.5	11.3
Polar maritime (Pm)	34.7	47.5
Polar continental (Pc)	1.4	0.7
Tropical maritime (Tm)	9.5	8.7
Tropical continental (Tc)	4.7	1.3
Anticyclones	24.3	13.8
Air in vicinity of fronts	11.3	11.8

Figure 5.2 Polar continental air mass crossing northeast England in winter

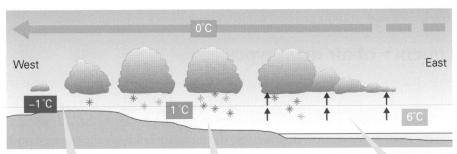

Air cools as it moves inland; conditions become stable; clouds dissipate and wintry showers die out

Rising air forms thick clouds — they bring wintry showers to the coast and eastern areas

Cold Pc air mass heated by contact with sea surface; instability; clouds form

Table 5.3 Weather associated with air mass types over land and sea

	Sea	Land
Arctic maritime (Am)	The air mass is cold (0 °C) and is heated by the warm ocean surface (4–9 °C) as it tracks south. As a result, the air mass is unstable	The land is colder than the Norwegian Sea. Thus the air mass cools as it tracks south overland and becomes increasingly stable
Polar maritime (Pm)	The air mass is cooler than the ocean surface and is therefore unstable over the ocean	Most of the land is cooler than the air mass. However, in Ireland and southwest England the air mass remains unstable
Polar continental (Pc)	The air mass is heated by the ocean. It becomes unstable during its passage across the North Sea	Land temperatures are often lower than the air mass. As a result the air mass gradually stabilises as it moves west across England and Scotland
Tropical maritime (Tm)	The air mass is warmer than the ocean surface and is therefore stable	Stability increases as the air mass moves northeast across the cooler land surface

Table 5.4 Air masses and weather types affecting the UK

Air mass	Source region and direction of approach	Stability	Winter weather	Summer weather
Arctic maritime (Am)	Arctic Ocean — northerly airstream	Unstable over the sea; becomes increasingly stable over land	Warmed by the ocean and unstable when reaches the UK. Northerly winds bring wintry showers to the north, and north-facing coasts. Cold, with below average temperatures and night-time frost. Cooling over the land often leads to clear skies and cold sunny conditions.	Rare in summer. In late spring and early summer outbreaks of Am air give unseasonably low temperatures (e.g. maximum 9–12°C).
Polar maritime (Pm)	Northern Canada, Greenland — westerly to northwesterly airstream	Unstable over the sea and land	Warmed as it crosses the ocean. Unstable and humid. Rain showers most frequent in the west, often dying out inland. Blustery northwest wind. Above average temperatures (c8°–10°C max). Clear skies at night with frost and fog inland.	Below average temperatures (c15–18°C max) with a cool northwesterly airflow. Some rain showers in the west. Instability may trigger convectional activity inland, with rain, hail and thunder.
Polar continental (Pc)	Eastern Europe, Siberia — easterly airstream	Unstable in winter; stable in summer	Very cold in its source region, but warmed as it tracks west. Warming due to contact with the North Sea leads to instability and wintry showers in eastern areas, especially near the coast. Inland, cooling causes instability to weaken; showers die out and skies clear. Low daytime maxima (0–3°C) with night-time frost.	The airmass originates in a warm continental interior and is cooled as it moves west. The North Sea cools and stabilises the air bringing advection fog and low stratus cloud to the North Sea coast. Inland, higher temperatures evaporate the fog and cloud to give clear skies, unbroken sunshine and temperatures into the mid-20s.
Tropical maritime (Tm)	Azores, Bermuda — southwesterly airstream	Stable	The airmass cools and becomes more humid as it tracks northeast across the ocean. Usually overcast (stratus), especially in the skies of western Britain, with drizzle on higher ground. Temperatures are above average and may reach 15°C even in mid-January.	Stratus often forms over the sea and there may be some advection fog particularly around southwest coasts. Inland the fog soon evaporates and most of the UK has clear skies with temperatures typically reaching 24–26°C.
Tropical continental (Tc)	North Africa and Mediterranean — southerly/southeasterly airstream	Stable in winter; unstable in summer	Rare in winter; winter weather is typically cloudy (stratus) and unusually mild	The air mass is dry and hot and gives heat wave conditions (max >30°C). Low humidity with clear skies. Thunderstorms may develop if temperatures rise sufficiently. Visibility often poor due to dust and smoke particles blown in from the near continent.

Activity 1

1 Study Figures 5.3 (a) and 5.3 (b). Sea-surface temperatures around the British Isles are near their maximum in mid-September and minimum in early March.

(a) Identify the four air masses indicated by the arrows on Figures 5.3 (a) and (b).

(b) State and explain the stability/instability of each air mass.

(c) Describe and explain the likely weather conditions associated with each air mass (see Table 5.4).

| Figure 5.3 | Air mass situations and sea-surface temperatures (SSTs) |

(a) mid-September

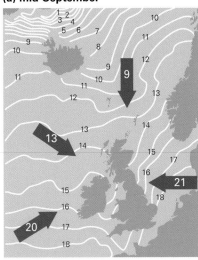

(b) early March

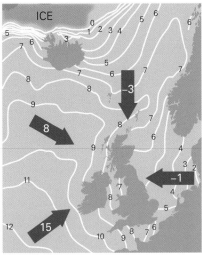

2 (a) Investigate the weather over the UK for a specific day or number of days when air masses (rather than depressions or anticyclones) dominate conditions. Compile information that includes air temperatures, sea-surface temperatures, synoptic charts, rainfall radar, satellite images etc. These data are available at:

www.metoffice.gov.uk/weather/uk/observations/ (air temperature/cloud cover/wind direction)

www.metoffice.gov.uk/weather/uk/radar/ (rainfall radar)

www.metoffice.gov.uk/satpics/latest_uk_ir.html (infrared satellite image)

www.sat.dundee.ac.uk/ (infrared and visible images)

www.weathercharts.org/ukmomslp.htm (synoptic charts)

www.wzkarten.de/pics/brack5.gif (sea-surface temperatures)

(b) Present an analysis of the weather, describing and explaining the conditions and regional variations. Base your analysis around a variety of charts, tables and images sourced from the internet.

6 Small- and medium-scale weather systems

Weather systems are atmospheric features such as tornadoes, depressions and anticyclones. These systems differ in size and lifespan. Small-scale features such as tornadoes develop rapidly and survive for just a few minutes. In contrast, large-scale systems (Chapter 7) like hurricanes and anticyclones grow, mature and decay over much longer periods of time, ranging from days to weeks (Figure 6.1).

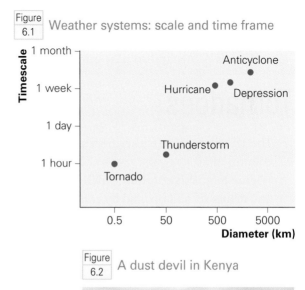

Figure 6.1 Weather systems: scale and time frame

Dust devils

Dust devils are small rotating columns of air, commonly found in hot arid and semi-arid areas (Figure 6.2). Unlike tornadoes, dust devils form from the ground up. Most last for just a few minutes and are rarely more than 500 m tall and 10 m wide. Dust devils form in response to intense solar heating of the Earth's surface and are most

Figure 6.2 A dust devil in Kenya

Wolfgang Kaehler/Alamy

frequent in the early afternoon when surface temperatures reach a peak. Surface heating causes instability as the air in contact with the ground becomes warmer than the air above. This results in small-scale convective circulation comprising plumes of rising hot air and falling plumes of cool air. If a gust of wind turns the convection cell on its side, the cell will spin horizontally and form a vortex as the air rotates around a vertical axis. As the warm air spirals upwards, low pressure at the surface draws cooler air into the column. The speed of rotation increases towards the centre of the axis.

Dust devils are only visible because they pick up dust particles and other debris. Small eddies like dust devils are found in most environments, but where vegetation cover is dense and soils are wet, they will not entrain dust and other debris and so pass unnoticed.

Tornadoes

The US National Weather Service defines a **tornado** as 'a violently rotating column of air in contact with the ground and pendant from a thunderstorm' (Figure 6.3). This column, which is funnel-shaped, is made visible by the dust and debris sucked up, and by condensation that forms cloud droplets. Within the column, wind speeds can reach $500\,\text{km}\,\text{h}^{-1}$, making tornadoes the most violent storms on Earth.

| Figure 6.3 | A tornado in the USA |

Chris White/Fotolia

Pressure inside the rotating column (known as a vortex or **mesocyclone**) can be 20% lower than the external air. This low pressure causes air close to the ground to rush in and spiral upwards. The combination of fierce winds and low pressure exerts enormous force on objects in the path of the vortex. Air is sucked from structures, causing them to implode. Meanwhile, flying debris, caught up in the vortex, presents a major hazard to life, limb and property.

Tornadoes range in width from a few metres (typically 20 to 100 m) to over a kilometre. Most last for 10 minutes or less and have storm tracks of between 2 and 5 km. Although their impact is localised, tornadoes are highly destructive because their energy is concentrated in such a small area.

Globally, tornadoes are mid-latitude phenomena. Conditions for tornado formation are most favourable in these latitudes, where cold polar air meets warm subtropical air along the polar front. Also, wind speed and wind direction in the mid-latitudes vary significantly with height, and this promotes rotation within storm cells. In an average year, about 1000 tornadoes are reported across the USA. The greatest concentrations are in the Midwest states, where cool dry air from the Rockies collides with warm moist air from the Gulf of Mexico (Figure 6.4). However, tornadoes are widespread. Even the UK experiences around 30 tornadoes a year, though they are far less intense than those in the USA.

Formation of tornadoes

The formation of tornadoes is still not fully understood and research by meteorologists is ongoing. What is known is the following:

- Tornadoes develop along the trailing edge of cold fronts, where cold dry air is located above warm, moist tropical air. This creates a situation of extreme instability.
- Cold fronts are boundaries between the warm and cold air. At a cold front, sharp contrasts in temperature lead to steep pressure gradients, causing winds to veer abruptly and change direction with height. These differences in pressure and

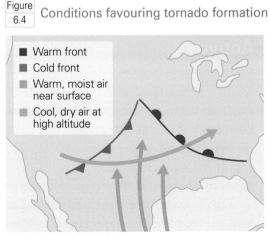

Figure 6.4 Conditions favouring tornado formation

- Warm front
- Cold front
- Warm, moist air near surface
- Cool, dry air at high altitude

wind direction create an invisible, horizontal spinning effect in the lower atmosphere (Figure 6.5).

- Powerful updraughts develop in the unstable air, which form towering cumulo-nimbus clouds and thunderstorms. The updraughts tilt the column of rotating air (3–9 km wide) from horizontal to vertical.
- Tornadoes form within the column of rotating air. As the column narrows, wind speeds accelerate due to the conservation of angular momentum until a funnel-shaped vortex extends from the cloud base to the ground.

| Figure 6.5 | Structure of a tornado |

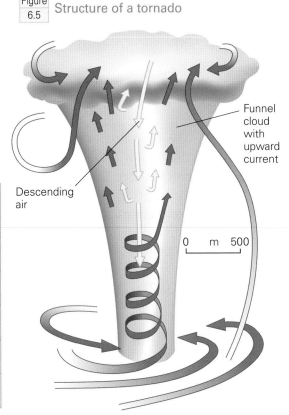

Funnel cloud with upward current

Descending air

0   m   500

| Table 6.1 | Fujita tornadic damage scale |

Level	Wind speed (km h^{-1})	Degree of damage
F0	97–117	Light damage
F1	118–180	Moderate damage
F2	181–253	Considerable damage
F3	254–332	Severe damage
F4	333–418	Devastating damage
F5	419–512	Incredible damage

Activity 1

Investigate tornado hazards in 'tornado alley' in the US Midwest. Look at (a) the causes of tornado formation in this area; (b) the times of year when tornadoes are most likely to form; (c) storm tracks; (d) tornado power.

Investigate a specific tornadic event in 'tornado alley' (e.g. 2 and 3 April 2006), including its causes and impacts.

Possible online sources include:

www.ncdc.noaa.gov/oa/climate/research/serrt/2006-tornadoes.html

www.spc.noaa.gov/climo/torn/2006deadlytorn.html

www.weatheronline.co.uk/reports/wxfacts/Tornado-Alley.htm

Thunderstorms

Thunderstorms are electrical storms generated within cumulo-nimbus clouds (Figure 6.6). They produce lightning, thunder and intense precipitation, including hail. Fairly localised events, thunderstorms have an average diameter of 25 km and generally last around 30 minutes.

Figure 6.6 Cumulo-nimbus clouds

Formation

The formation of thunderstorms requires a deep unstable layer in the troposphere allowing air to rise freely to heights of 10–15 km. Air rises in updraughts, which may reach speeds of up to 80 km h^{-1}. The rising air cools adiabatically, and condensation results in cloud formation and a release of latent heat. This latent heat provides energy that generates further uplift and becomes a self-generating process.

The triggers that cause air to rise vertically include:
- heating of the surface by the sun, creating warm parcels of buoyant air
- high ground forcing air aloft, which often then rises freely
- frontal surfaces, especially cold fronts, where warm air is undercut by cold air and forced upwards

Thunder and lightning

Thunderstorms only develop where (a) clouds extend well above the freezing level; (b) precipitation occurs; and (c) the cloud axis is almost vertical, with little wind shear.

Lightning is caused by the separation of electrical charges in storm clouds. The processes leading to this separation are not fully understood. However, it is clear that positively charged ice particles concentrate in the upper parts of thunderstorm clouds, while negatively charged ice particles and raindrops migrate towards the cloud base. The result is an electric field within the cloud. If the field is strong, it overcomes the frictional resistance of the air, releasing a massive transfer of electrons as a giant spark or lightning. Lightning may occur between clouds, within clouds or between a cloud and the ground surface. With lightning reaching temperatures of 22 000 °C, air in its vicinity is superheated, expands rapidly and creates thunder.

Precipitation

Precipitation in thunderstorms is usually short-lived and intense. Precipitation intensities often exceed 30 mm an hour and create problems of flash flooding (see Chapter 8). Small balls of ice or hail are often precipitated in thunderstorms. Powerful updraughts carry water droplets above the freezing level, where they form ice particles. Collisions between the ice particles and supercooled water droplets cause the particles to grow. Where the updraughts are particularly strong, large particles of ice and hail may be held in suspension for up to 30 minutes as they circulate within the cloud. Eventually the hailstones either become too large to resist gravity or the updraughts weaken and they fall from the cloud. Depending on temperatures in the lower atmosphere, the particles may reach the ground as hail or, if they melt, form torrential rain. A typical example occurred in Exeter on 6 June 2009, when a thunderstorm deposited over 27 mm of rain in an hour.

Table 6.2 Hailstone size and speed of updraughts in thunderstorm clouds

Hailstone size is a good indicator of the power and severity of a thunderstorm because the larger the hailstones, the more powerful the updraughts needed to keep them in suspension (Table 6.2).

	Diameter (cm)	Updraught speed (km h^{-1})
One penny	2	65
Golfball	4.3	100
Baseball	11.4	160

Cold downdraughts

A feature of the later stages of thunderstorm development is the onset of cold downdraughts of air, which spread out at the surface to give strong gusts and squally winds. Cold dense air from high levels within the storm sinks to the surface. Falling rain also exerts a frictional drag, which pulls cold air towards the surface.

Stages in the development of thunderstorms

Thunderstorms evolve in three stages: an initial cumulus stage; a mature stage; and a dissipating stage. The main features of each stage are described in Table 6.3.

Table 6.3 Stages in the development of a thunderstorm

1 Cumulus stage	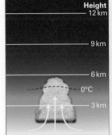	In this stage, unstable warm air breaks away from the surface and rises in a thermal. Cumulus cloud forms as the air cools and passes the condensation level. As the water vapour condenses, it releases latent heat, which reinforces the updraughts. No precipitation or lightning occurs. Updraughts are so vigorous that any rain, hail or snow is held in suspension
2 Mature stage	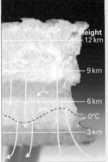	The mature stage of a thunderstorm is reached when precipitation starts to occur. Updraughts reach their maximum velocity and cold drowndraughts reach the surface just before the onset of precipitation. At this stage, the tops of the thunderstorm clouds may reach the level of the tropopause. Cloud at this height comprises ice crystals and, blown by strong winds, spreads out to form a characteristic anvil shape. The thunderstorm develops to its maximum intensity. Lightning reaches a climax, precipitation is at its heaviest, and simultaneous updraughts and downdraughts are at their strongest
3 Dissipating stage	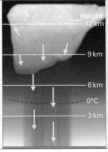	In the dissipation stage, the thunderstorm is dominated by downdraughts. The supply of warm moist air that feeds the storm becomes exhausted. Cool air carried to the ground by the downdraught also cuts off the supply of inflow of warm air. Thus updraughts disappear and the thunderstorm quickly dissipates

Squall lines

Squall lines are bands of thunderstorms that have a common lifting mechanism. The most common lifting mechanism is a cold front in a depression. The classic squall line develops parallel to, and on the leading edge of, a cold front. As the front advances, continuous uplift of moist, unstable air generates new thunderstorm cells. The structure of a squall line in cross-section is shown in Figure 6.7.

| Figure 6.7 | Cross-section through a squall line |

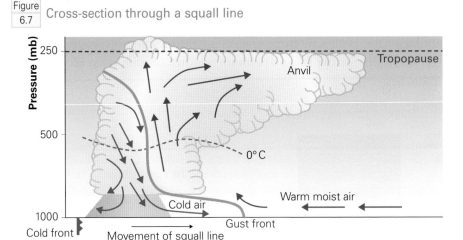

Supercell thunderstorms

Supercells are large isolated thunderstorms, which, unlike ordinary (multi-cell) thunderstorms, remain active for several hours (see Chapter 8). They bring extreme weather conditions, including violent downbursts of cold air, golfball-size hailstones, flash floods and tornadoes. Not surprisingly, supercells pose major hazards to the public and to aviation. Supercells are rare in the UK, but common during summer in temperate continental regions such as the US Midwest, where they often spawn tornadoes.

Supercell development depends on a number of atmospheric conditions:
- a layer of warm moist air at and near the ground surface
- cold air aloft
- a deep unstable layer, often extending to the tropopause

Unlike ordinary thunderstorms, supercells also need strong **wind shear** aloft (i.e. winds blowing from different directions). Wind shear is responsible for the formation of the spinning column of rising air or mesocyclone, which is the trademark feature of supercells.

Supercells are long-lasting because warm rising air is segregated from cold downdraughts and precipitation. In ordinary thunderstorms, precipitation and cold air eventually fall into the warm updraughts, suppressing them and cutting off the storm's energy supply. In contrast, supercells receive a continuous supply of water vapour and energy, allowing them to survive and self-generate for 4 or 5 hours.

7 Large-scale weather systems

In this chapter we investigate the physical processes and weather patterns associated with large-scale weather systems such as mid-latitude depressions, tropical cyclones and anticyclones.

Depressions

Depressions are large, travelling low-pressure systems that dominate the weather and climate in middle latitudes. These areas of low pressure are up to 3000 km in diameter and are easily identified on weather charts by their roughly circular pattern of isobars and frontal systems (Figure 7.1). In the northern hemisphere, winds rotate anticlockwise in depressions and gradually spiral in towards the low-pressure centre. Frontal systems are boundaries between contrasting air masses within depressions. Physical processes are most active in the vicinity of the fronts, and give rise to thick cloud and precipitation. Depressions play a crucial role in the Earth's energy budget, transferring warm air in the tropics to higher latitudes.

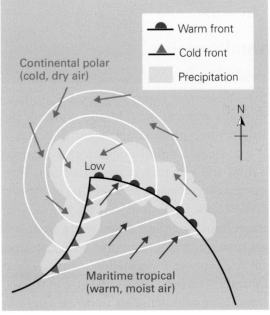

Figure 7.1 Mid-latitude storm — a depression model

The formation of depressions (cyclogenesis)

Depressions develop on the polar front jet stream, the narrow belt of fast-moving air that encircles mid-latitudes around the height of the tropopause. A simplified sequence of events leading to depression formation is as follows:

- Air moves from west to east in the jet stream at variable speeds, slowing in places, accelerating in others. These changes in wind speed are related to the wave-like pattern of upper-level ridges and troughs followed by the jet stream (see Figure 1.7 on page 11).
- The jet stream accelerates as it flows round a trough and decelerates round a ridge. This is because the centripetal force due to the wind's curved path acts in the same direction as the pressure gradient force in a trough (and in the opposite direction in a ridge).
- Acceleration leads to upper-air divergence and low pressure at the surface.
- Warmer air, to the south of the polar front, is sucked into the surface low-pressure area and rises through the lower atmosphere. This forms the warm sector. Cold polar air forms the upper-level trough and the cold sector.
- The outcome is the formation and deepening of surface depressions.
- Surface depressions migrate across the Atlantic, steered by the polar front jet stream.

Frontal systems

Depressions form as waves along the polar front, where cold and warm air masses meet (see Figure 7.2). Because air masses do not mix easily, boundaries or fronts separate the cold and warm air in depressions. Sharp contrasts in temperature, pressure and wind direction occur at these frontal surfaces. Warm air, of tropical origin, forms a narrow wedge that occupies between a third and a quarter of the depression. This is the **warm sector**. Most of the depression comprises polar air and is sometimes referred to as the **cold sector**.

The boundary forming the leading edge of the warm air is known as the **warm front**. The slope of the warm front is shallow (Figure 7.2). Here warm air rises gently above colder, denser air and forms clouds that fill most of the troposphere. Precipitation falls steadily at the warm front and often lasts for several hours. The trailing edge of the warm sector is marked by the cold front. Here cold dense air undercuts the warm sector, forcing the warm air to rise abruptly and more steeply than at the warm front. Once again there is extensive cloud development and precipitation. Precipitation is usually heavier than at the warm front but shorter in duration.

Air behind the cold front is faster moving than air in the warm sector. This is because a slight anticyclonic curvature often develops behind the cold

Figure 7.2 The stages of, and cross-section through, a depression

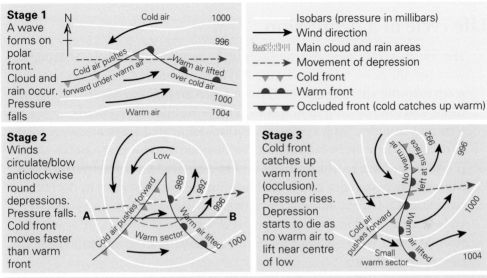

Stage 1
A wave forms on polar front. Cloud and rain occur. Pressure falls

Cold air pushes forward under warm air
Warm air lifted over cold air
Warm air

- Isobars (pressure in millibars)
- → Wind direction
- Main cloud and rain areas
- ---→ Movement of depression
- Cold front
- Warm front
- Occluded front (cold catches up warm)

Stage 2
Winds circulate/blow anticlockwise round depressions. Pressure falls. Cold front moves faster than warm front

Low
Cold air pushes forward
Warm sector
Warm air lifted
A — B

Stage 3
Cold front catches up warm front (occlusion). Pressure rises. Depression starts to die as no warm air to lift near centre of low

No warm air Left at surface
Cold air pushes forward
Warm air lifted
Small warm sector

Cross-section through a depression

Section **A–B** for stage 2

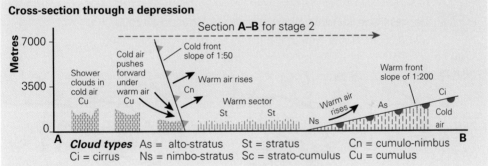

Metres: 7000, 3500, 0

Shower clouds in cold air Cu
Cold air pushes forward under warm air Cu
Cold front slope of 1:50
Warm air rises Cn
Warm sector St St
Ns
Warm air rises
Warm front slope of 1:200
As Ci
Cold air

A *Cloud types* As = alto-stratus St = stratus Cn = cumulo-nimbus B
Ci = cirrus Ns = nimbo-stratus Sc = strato-cumulus Cu = cumulus

front, making the winds supergeostrophic (see Chapter 4). As it advances, the warm sector narrows and is eventually lifted bodily above the ground to form an **occlusion** (Figure 7.3). Occlusions develop outwards from the

Figure 7.3 Warm and cold occlusions

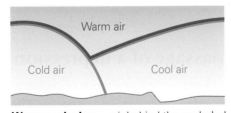

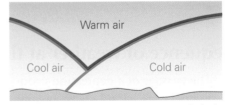

Warm occlusion — air behind the occluded front is colder than the air ahead of it

Cold occlusion — air behind the occluded front is warmer than the air ahead of it

centre of depressions along the warm front. Like warm fronts and cold fronts, occlusions are associated with thick cloud and precipitation.

Life cycle of a depression

The life cycle of a typical depression takes around 4 or 5 days. Starting as waves on the polar front (see Figure 7.2) in the western Atlantic, depressions reach maturity after a couple of days, and then occlude (see Figure 7.2) before filling and disappearing from weather charts over northern Eurasia.

In mid-latitudes, long spells of weather dominated by depressions tend to develop when the North Atlantic Oscillation (NAO) is in a positive phase (i.e. there are large pressure differences between the Azores and Iceland). This happened in November 2009, which was the wettest November in the UK on record (see Chapter 9). In these circumstances, depressions occur as 'families', with three or four in various stages of development strung out across the North Atlantic from eastern Canada to northeast Europe, and following an easterly track (Figure 7.4).

| Figure 7.4 | Depressions: synoptic charts for 18–19 November 2009: (a) 00.00 18 November 2009; (b) 00.00 19 November 2009 |

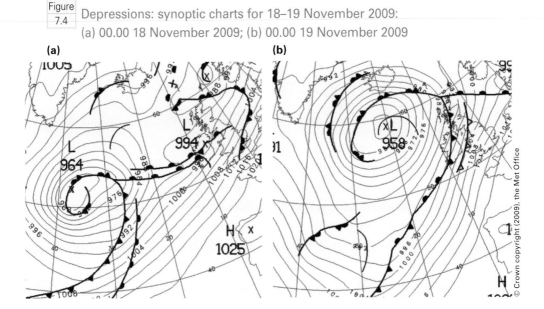

Sequence of weather at the passage of a depression

The passage of a depression produces a characteristic sequence of changes in temperature, cloud cover, precipitation, wind direction and pressure. These are summarised in Table 7.1.

Table 7.1   Weather changes with the passage of a depression

	1 Approach of warm front	2 Passage of warm front	3 Behind warm front
Pressure	Falls steadily	Stabilises	No change
Temperature	No change	Rises	No change
Cloud cover	Cloud thickens from cirrus, to alto-stratus and alto-cumulus, to nimbo-stratus and strato-cumulus	Thick cloud at low altitude	Cloud disperses; sky clears
Precipitation	Begins slowly and continues steadily for several hours	Ceases	No precipitation
Wind direction	No change	Veers	No change

	4 Approach of cold front	5 Passage of cold front	6 Behind cold front
Pressure	No change	Rises abruptly	No change
Temperature	No change	Falls	No change
Cloud cover	Cloud thickens — nimbo-stratus and cumulo-nimbus	Thick cloud at low altitude	Sky clears abruptly; individual cumuliform clouds develop in unstable Pm air
Precipitation	Heavy precipitation	Heavy precipitation; chance of thunder	Intermittent showers in unstable airstream
Wind direction	No change	Veers	No change

Activity 1

Study the weather charts for 18–19 November 2009 (Figure 7.4).

Describe and explain the likely weather changes across the UK during this 24-hour period.

Tropical cyclones

Tropical cyclones are powerful storms that develop over warm oceans, between latitudes 7° and 20°. They are best known as **hurricanes**, which is the name given to them in the Atlantic region. They are called **typhoons** in east Asia and Australia, and **cyclones** in south Asia. Tropical cyclones cannot develop close to the equator because the Coriolis effect is too small to generate a spinning motion in the air.

The anatomy of tropical cyclones

Tropical cyclones, like mid-latitude depressions, are areas of low pressure which are circular in plan, when viewed from satellites or on weather charts (see Figure 10.4 on page 101). Averaging around 650 km in diameter, they are smaller than mid-latitude depressions, but much more intense. Tropical cyclones are upgraded from tropical storms when sustained wind speeds reach 119 km h^{-1}. However, the most intense cyclones can generate constant winds in excess of 300 km h^{-1}.

In the northern hemisphere, surface winds circulate anticlockwise around tropical cyclones and spiral in towards the low-pressure centre. Winds strengthen as they converge on the centre of the storm due to conservation of angular momentum (see Chapter 4). Towering cumulo-nimbus clouds and thunderstorms form two or three circular concentric bands around the central core. Throughout the lower atmosphere, air rises vertically, creating low pressure at the surface and high pressure at upper levels (Figure 7.5). At upper levels the air diverges, complementing the convergence near the surface. The centre of the storm is known as the **eye**. This warm core, around 50 km in diameter, is calm and often cloud-free. Within it, air sinks towards the surface, warming the atmosphere by compression and preventing cloud formation.

| Figure 7.5 | The anatomy of a tropical cyclone |

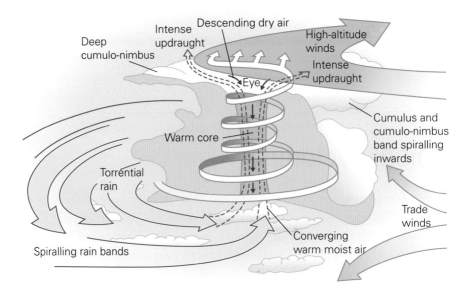

Bordering the eye is the eye wall, a ring of tall thunderstorms that produce heavy rain and fierce winds. This is most destructive part of the storm. Curved bands of clouds surround the eye wall and trail away in a spiral fashion. These cloud bands also produce heavy bursts of rain and strong winds.

Development and decay of tropical cyclones

A number of favourable weather and ocean conditions are needed for the development of tropical cyclones:

- high humidity and therefore plenty of water vapour
- light winds which allow vertical cloud development (i.e. little or no wind shear)
- convergent winds at low levels and divergent winds aloft
- sea-surface temperatures (SSTs) of at least 26–27 °C and a deep warm-water layer of 60–70 m. This warm layer prevents cold water rising to the surface and killing the system

These conditions are found in the summer and early autumn in the tropical north Atlantic and north Pacific oceans. As a result, the hurricane season in the northern hemisphere lasts from June to late November. By December, ocean surface waters are too cool to generate hurricanes.

The first signs of a developing tropical cyclone are thunderstorm clusters that form over the ocean. In the tropical north Atlantic, these disturbances form as waves embedded in the easterly jet stream and originate off the coast of west Africa.

Given favourable conditions, clusters of tropical thunderstorms become more structured and begin to develop an anticlockwise spin. Surface pressure falls as air, heated from below, starts to rise. As the air rises and cools, condensation releases latent heat, warming the atmosphere and triggering further instability and rising air. This has a feedback effect (Figure 7.6), lowering

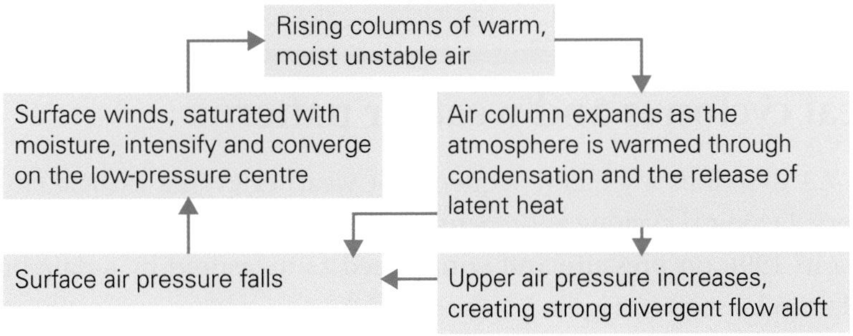

Figure 7.6 Positive feedback driving the development of a tropical cyclone

pressure further and causing surface air, saturated with moisture from evaporation over the ocean, to *converge* even more vigorously. Meanwhile, the columns of rising air create high pressure near the tropopause. This leads to rapid *divergence* of air near the top of the storm, which intensifies low pressure at the surface. As a result, the central area of a tropical cyclone behaves like a giant chimney: low pressure at the surface draws air inwards, while high pressure aloft forces the air outwards. In this way, the hurricane gets a constant supply of vapour — the energy that drives the storm.

Although tropical cyclones take weeks to form, once they reach maturity they may disappear in just a few days. Rapid decay takes place when a storm:

- moves over cooler water and loses its supply of warm, moist air
- moves over land, where it abruptly loses its power source — warm, moist air
- moves into an area where either the large-scale flow aloft is subsiding or where there is strong wind shear

The Saffir–Simpson scale

The Saffir–Simpson scale (Table 7.2) defines the intensity of hurricanes in terms of the level of damage caused by winds and flooding. Hurricanes are graded from 1 (weakest) to 5 (strongest). The scale takes account of a hurricane's central pressure, maximum sustained winds, and storm-surge levels. Sustained wind speed is the critical factor, as storm surges are also affected by the slope of the continental shelf in the landfall region. Categories 3, 4, and 5 are considered as major (intense) hurricanes, capable of inflicting great damage and loss of life.

Table 7.2 The Saffir–Simpson scale

Scale number	1	2	3	4	5
Central pressure (mb)	>980	965–979	945–964	920–944	<920
Wind speed (km h^{-1})	119–153	154–177	178–209	210–249	>249
Storm surge (m)	1.20–1.80	1.81–2.70	2.71–4.00	4.01–5.50	>5.50
Damage	Minimal	Moderate	Extensive	Extreme	Catastrophic

Tropical cyclones and weather patterns

Table 7.3 describes a general sequence of weather events associated with a category 2 tropical cyclone approaching a coastal area. The effect of Hurricane Bertha in 1996 on pressure and wind speed as measured by a data buoy off Florida can be seen in Figure 7.7 (page 68).

Table
7.3 Sequence of weather changes associated with the passage of a tropical cyclone

Approach of the eye of the storm	
36–96 hours before landfall	No apparent signs of a storm. The barometer is steady, winds are light and variable, and fair-weather cumulus clouds appear
24–36 hours	The first signs of the storm appear. Pressure falls slightly, the wind increases gradually to $30\,km\,h^{-1}$, and cirrus clouds appear. Eventually the sky becomes overcast with high cirro-stratus cloud
12–24 hours	Small low clouds appear overhead. Pressure falls more rapidly (0.2–$0.5\,mb\,h^{-1}$) and wind speeds increase to around $50\,km\,h^{-1}$ and then to $65\,km\,h^{-1}$. Low clouds thicken and bring driving rain squalls with gusty winds. It is hard to stand against the wind
6–12 hours	The rain squalls are more frequent and the cloud base lowers. Pressure falls at a rate of 1–$1.5\,mb\,h^{-1}$. The wind begins to howl at hurricane force ($120\,km\,h^{-1}$). Rain is constant and driven horizontally by the winds. It is impossible to stand upright outside without bracing yourself
1–6 hours	The rain becomes heavier. Wind speeds exceed $150\,km\,h^{-1}$ and pressure falls at $2\,mb\,h^{-1}$
The eye	Just as the storm reaches its peak, the winds begin to slacken. The rain ends abruptly, clouds clear and blue sky appears. The barometer continues falling at $3\,mb\,h^{-1}$. Eventually the winds fall to near calm. The air is uncomfortably warm and humid. Huge walls of cloud appear on every side, brilliant white in the sunlight. Pressure stops falling and begins to rise rapidly. Winds begin to pick up slightly and the clouds on the far side of the eye wall loom overhead
After the passage of the eye of the storm	
1–6 hours	The sky darkens and the wind and rain returns with the same intensity as before the eye. Pressure continues to rise rapidly and winds reach over $150\,km\,h^{-1}$
6–12 hours	Wind speeds fall to $140\,km\,h^{-1}$. The rain becomes squally as the winds diminish further. The cloud base lifts and pressure rises at $1\,mb\,h^{-1}$. The wind still howls at near hurricane force
12–24 hours	Low clouds disperse and the high clouds reappear. Pressure rises slowly ($0.2\,mb\,h^{-1}$) and wind speeds fall to $50\,km\,h^{-1}$.
24–36 hours	Cirrus and cirro-stratus clouds disappear and the sky clears. Winds slacken to just $15\,km\,h^{-1}$ and pressure remains more or less constant

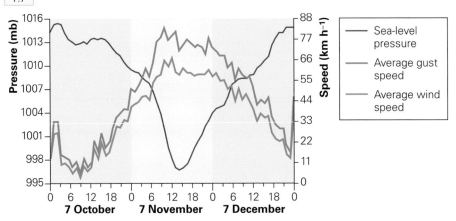

Figure 7.7 Pressure and wind speed: time series plot for Hurricane Bertha, 1996

Activity 2

(a) Plot the pressure and wind speed data for 29 August 2005 for Bayou La Branche (Table 7.4) as a line chart in Excel. Use separate scales (one for pressure and one for wind speed) for the primary and secondary vertical axes. The data relate to the 8–9 hours before Hurricane Katrina made landfall near New Orleans. Bayou La Branche is located 20 km to the west of New Orleans.

(b) Describe and explain the relationship between pressure and wind speed in Table 7.4.

(c) Give possible explanations for the time trends in pressure and wind speed in Table 7.4.

Table 7.4 Bayou La Branche: changes in pressure and wind speed with the approach of Hurricane Katrina (29 August 2005)

Time	Pressure (mb)	Sustained wind speed (km h^{-1})	Time	Pressure (mb)	Sustained wind speed (km h^{-1})
03.00	1001.0	63.7	07.30	992.9	79.9
03.30	1000.7	63.0	08.00	991.6	70.6
04.00	1000.0	66.6	08.30	990.2	95.4
04.30	995.5	70.2	09.00	986.7	94.7
05.00	998.6	71.3	09.30	986.2	86.8
05.30	998.1	65.9	10.00	983.8	95.4
06.00	997.3	63.4	10.30	980.5	109.4
06.30	996.0	67.3	11.00	977.2	110.9
07.00	994.8	68.4	11.30	976.9	113.0

Activity 3

Study Figure 7.8, which shows rainfall totals at 60-minute intervals at Newton, Mississippi, with the approach of Hurricane Katrina (see the location of Newton, and Katrina's track, in Figure 7.9). Describe and explain (a) the intensity of rainfall; (b) the influence of the hurricane on the time trend of rainfall at Newton.

Figure 7.8 Rainfall totals at 60-minute intervals at Newton, Mississippi, with the approach of Hurricane Katrina

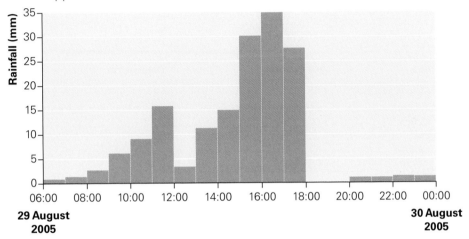

Figure 7.9 The track of Hurricane Katrina

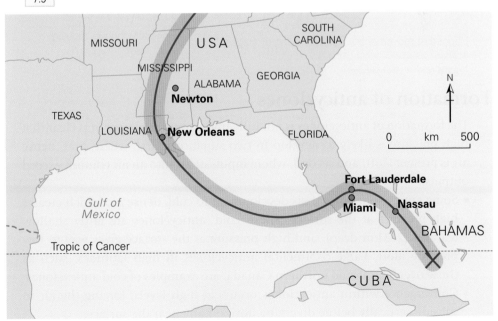

Anticyclones

Anticyclones are areas of high pressure, typically in the range 1020–1050 mb. On weather charts, they have a roughly circular pattern of isobars with pressure increasing towards the centre. At the surface and in the northern hemisphere, light winds spiral outwards in a clockwise direction (Table 7.5). On average anticyclones control the weather in the British Isles around one day in four.

Table 7.5 The contrasting features of anticyclones and depressions

Feature	Anticyclone	Depression
Surface pressure	High	Low
Wind direction	Anticyclonic (clockwise*)	Cyclonic (anticlockwise*)
Airflow	Diverges at surface (converges aloft)	Converges at surface (diverges aloft)
Vertical air motion	Subsides	Rises
Wind speed	Weak	Moderate to strong
Precipitation	Generally dry	Wet
Cloudiness	Stratus or no cloud	Cloudy
Stability	Stable air, with a subsidence inversion aloft	May be unstable
Temperature gradient	Little temperature contrast across the high	Strong temperature contrasts, especially at the fronts
Speed of movement	Slow-moving or stagnant	Generally mobile, moving west–east

* in the northern hemisphere

Formation of anticyclones

The formation of anticyclones is not fully understood. However, it is clear that high pressure is likely to develop in two situations: first, where cold, dense air is present aloft; and second, where inputs of air into an air column exceed outputs.

- Some anticyclones owe their development to cold, dense air, which creates high pressure at the surface. These 'cold' anticyclones are fairly shallow features (2–3 km deep), and high pressure at the surface gives way to low pressure aloft. Large continental anticyclones in high latitudes, such as those over Siberia and northern Canada, are examples of cold anticyclones.
- Convergence within anticyclones occurs at high levels, forcing the air to subside vertically before diverging horizontally near the surface.

- Warm anticyclones have a core of unusually warm air that extends to the upper troposphere. They are associated with high pressure both at the surface and aloft.
- The subtropical high-pressure belt situated on the poleward limb of the Hadley cell is an example of a warm anticyclone. Mobile warm anticyclones develop in mid-latitudes on the Rossby waves (see Chapter 1), which form a series of ridges and troughs in the upper air. Winds accelerate and decelerate in waves. Where the waves swing towards the equator, the jet stream slows, leading to convergence and an increase in air mass. As a result, air is forced vertically downwards towards the Earth's surface (Figure 7.10). Near the surface, the air spreads out in all directions (divergence).
- Because the rate of convergence exceeds the rate of divergence, high pressure develops at the surface. The Rossby waves steer mobile anticyclones, the latter often appearing as ridges of high pressure between adjacent depressions.

| Figure 7.10 | Cross-section through an anticyclone |

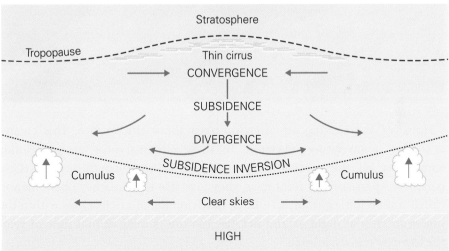

Anticyclonic weather in the UK

Anticyclones bring settled weather conditions and occasionally extreme temperatures and rainfall (see Chapter 11). Once established, anticyclones may persist for days or even weeks, making conditions even more extreme.

Figure 7.10 shows that air subsides vertically in anticyclones throughout the troposphere. This is due to the convergence of air aloft. Subsidence is the key to understanding the weather patterns associated with anticyclones. As the air sinks towards the surface, it is compressed by rising pressure and warms (adiabatic warming). Warming prevents cloud formation, so the troposphere remains clear. As a result, anticyclones nearly always bring dry conditions. If subsidence reaches the surface, clear skies will result in lots of sunshine and night-time frost (and fog) in winter (Figure 7.11).

| Figure 7.11 | Clear, cold anticyclonic weather in the English Lake District |

Michael Raw

However, the sinking air often diverges above the surface. This creates a shallow temperature inversion. In these circumstances, stratus clouds sometimes fill the inversion layer to give overcast conditions. If these conditions persist for several days, they give rise to a weather phenomenon called 'anticyclonic gloom'. In winter, radiation fog often develops within the inversion layer at night — and because the sun is weak at that time of year, the fog may remain all day.

In summer, air heated by contact with the ground sometimes results in a shallow, unstable layer just a kilometre or so in depth. Within this layer, convection can generate small fair-weather cumulus clouds.

Anticyclonic blocking

Slow-moving anticyclones often establish themselves over northwest Europe and remain stationary for several days or even weeks. In winter, these anticyclones may be a western extension of the huge anticyclone over Eurasia.

In summer, they are more likely to be linked to the Azores anticyclone in mid-Atlantic. **Blocking** disrupts the normal westerly (zonal) flow, deflecting frontal systems and depressions either south of their normal track into the Mediterranean or north across northern Norway. When blocking occurs in winter, the weather in the UK is dominated by northerly and easterly airflows and extreme temperatures. Sub-zero temperatures, including daytime frosts, are common. In summer, airflows from the south and southeast sometimes produce exceptionally high temperatures and heatwaves. Sunshine amounts during anticyclonic episodes are less predictable and depend on wind direction and humidity. Air near the surface, which is cooled and humid, may produce masses of low stratus cloud. Drier air is more likely to result in cloudless skies and unbroken sunshine.

Blocking also brings unusually dry weather. Droughts (see Chapter 11) may develop, especially in summer when evapotranspiration is high. A prolonged block in 1995, when rainfall in the UK was only 43% of the average, was responsible for the driest summer for 229 years.

Figure 7.12 shows a typical blocking situation in western Europe in winter. In this example, blocking lasted for 2 weeks. During this time very little rainfall was recorded and there was a lengthy cold spell. Clear night skies produced sharp frosts: –8.7 °C at Redhill (Surrey) on 25 January and –7.5 °C at Shap Fell (Cumbria) on 29 January. Freezing fog was also widespread.

| Figure 7.12 | Anticyclone blocking, 27 January 2006 |

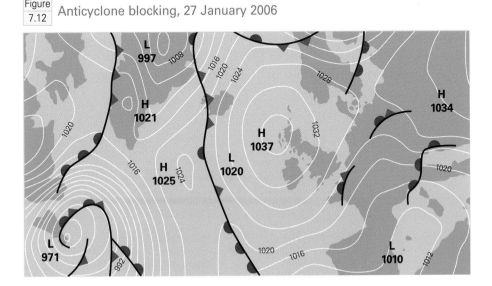

8 Thunderstorms, tornadoes and extreme weather hazards

Different weather systems are associated with characteristic patterns and intensities of weather. Of particular importance are extreme weather events — thunderstorms, gales, blizzards, torrential rain, heatwaves — which directly threaten people, the economy and society.

Hazardous weather events

Extreme weather events give rise to natural hazards such as severe hailstorms, droughts and blizzards. Some weather hazards are indirectly related to extreme weather. For example, floods and landslides may result from heavy rainfall. However, extreme weather is not in itself a hazard. What makes these natural events hazardous is the damaging effect they have on people, infrastructure and economic activities (Figure 8.1). When natural hazards cause large numbers of fatalities and injuries and/or major economic losses, they are known as **natural disasters**.

Figure 8.1 The occurrence of weather hazards

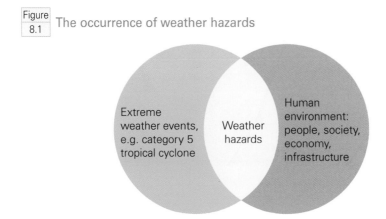

Extreme weather events, e.g. category 5 tropical cyclone

Weather hazards

Human environment: people, society, economy, infrastructure

The risks posed by extreme weather depend on the physical **exposure** and **vulnerability** of society to weather hazards. Physical exposure is usually expressed in terms of the number of people living in areas at risk from hazardous weather events, and the frequency with which such events occur. However, similar levels of exposure can result in different degrees of risk. For example, a category 5 tropical cyclone is likely to have a greater impact in Bangladesh than in Florida. The reason is that risk is also influenced by the second factor — vulnerability. Vulnerability covers a range of economic, social, technological and political aspects. Poverty, at both individual and national levels, has the biggest influence on vulnerability. Poor people and poor nations are the least able to protect themselves from the adverse effects of major weather hazards.

Risks can both increase and decrease depending on human activities and adaptive strategies. Deforestation, for example, can greatly increase the flood hazards induced by heavy rain. Equally, the potential flood risks from extreme rainfall events can be mitigated by planning and the building of flood-control structures. However, such mitigating action is less likely to be an option in poorer societies.

Table 8.1 Weather systems and related hazards

	Extreme precipitation and related hazards	High winds and related hazards	Cold spells and heatwaves and related hazards	Drought and related hazards
Thunderstorms	*			
Tornadoes		*		
Tropical cyclones	*	*		
Depressions	*	*		
Anticyclones			*	*

Thunderstorm hazards

The Biescas flash flood, northern Spain, 1996

Causes

On the evening of 7 August 1996, the Arás river basin near Biescas in the central Pyrenees (Figure 8.2) was hit by a powerful thunderstorm. The thunderstorm, which showed some of the characteristics of a supercell (see Chapter 6, page 58) remained more or less stationary for nearly 2 hours. Rainfall intensity reached $100 \, mm \, h^{-1}$ and the storm dumped around 250 mm of rain on parts of the catchment in less than 3 hours (Figure 8.3). This extreme rainfall event produced peak flows on the River Arás of 500 cumecs (1 cumec = $1 \, m^3 \, s^{-1}$) — remarkable for a small catchment covering just 19 km². What triggered the thunderstorm was intense solar heating of the ground. This, combined with cold air, created extreme instability. Upslope winds in the mountains also contributed to the formation of deep thunderstorm clouds. In addition to the exceptional rainfall, the steep slopes of the catchment and impermeable geology had a direct influence on the severity of the flood.

| Figure 8.2 | Peak flows: the Arás river basin near Biescas in the central Pyrenees |

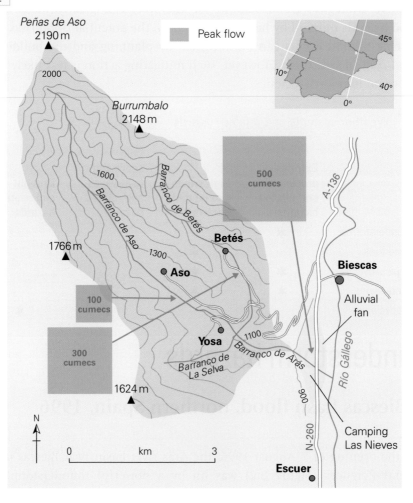

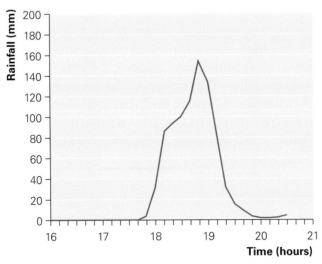

Figure 8.3 Rainfall intensity at Yosa in the Arás river basin (10-minute intervals)

Impact

The thunderstorm on 7 August produced a violent flash flood. The flood-waters were mixed with huge amounts of sediment, trees and other material — the characteristics of a **debris flow**. Sediment loads were also increased by the collapse of a series of sediment traps in the Arás channel, downstream of its confluence with the Betés.

The thunderstorm resulted in a major flood disaster. A flash flood struck the Las Nieves campsite near Biescas (see Figure 8.2) at 19.15 without warning, sending a giant wave of water, mud, rocks and uprooted trees crashing through the site. Out of the 650 people at the campsite, 87 were killed and 200 injured. One British family survived the storm in a tree, the parents clutching their two young children, as water rose more than 1 m high. Tents, mobile homes and cars were swept several kilometres downstream, and some bodies were later recovered up to 15 km away.

The morning after the flood, a *New York Times* reporter described the campsite as 'a battlefield strewn with cars, mobile homes and trees that had been torn from the ground. Twisted mobile homes and jeeps filled with mud and rock lay strewn over what had once been a typical camping area'.

Response

Some 500 emergency rescue workers, including divers and firefighters, backed by helicopter teams and army mountain units, took part in the search for survivors and bodies. Most of the survivors were taken to a sports centre in Biescas. Others were housed in hotels, police stations and private houses in the area. Several days after the disaster, bodies were still being recovered several kilometres downstream.

Flash floods develop rapidly and are difficult to predict, making early warning and evacuation almost impossible. Risk management by planners and local authorities should aim to mitigate the effects of such floods by avoiding development in areas at most risk. The Aragón regional government was heavily criticised for approving the location of the Las Nieves campsite on an **alluvial fan**. The alluvial had itself been formed by sediment deposited by previous flash floods and should have been recognised as an area of high risk. The regional government argued that the torrential rain that triggered the flood was impossible to foresee and denied that its planners could have predicted the disaster.

In December 2005, a High Court judge ruled that the central government and the regional government of Aragón should pay nearly €12 million compensation to the families of the 87 people who died in the flood. The decision hinged on the fact that the authorities had ignored a written report from experts detailing the risks involved in permitting the campsite to be located on the alluvial fan.

Activity 1

(a) Assess the level of exposure of the Las Nieves campsite to flash-flood hazards.

(b) To what extent was the Biescas flash flood a natural disaster rather than one caused by human activity?

(c) Investigate the causes of the Boscastle flash flood in Cornwall in 2004 and write a report comparing and contrasting the causes of the Biescas and Boscastle events. Start your search for information at: **www.metoffice.gov.uk/education/teens/casestudy_boscastle.html**

Hailstorm hazards

Hailstorms are common weather hazards, especially in temperate continental regions such as northern Texas and the US Midwest. Hail can destroy crops in just a few minutes and every year in the USA hailstorms cause damage to crops and property costing millions of dollars. Meanwhile, large hailstones can cause serious injury and even endanger life. The damage caused by severe hailstorms is evident in the description of the storm that hit Hale County in northwest Texas in October 2007 (Figure 8.4).

Figure 8.4   Article adapted from *Southwest Farm Press,* 1 November 2007

Devastating hailstorm strikes Hale County, north Texas

A severe storm, packing wind gusts up to 120 km h^{-1}, heavy rain, and devastating hail swept through the western part of Hale County on October 10th, leaving behind hail accumulations of 13 cm, rainfall amounts exceeding 75 mm, and some US$15 million in crop losses.

"I have not seen such a destructive hailstorm since June 1997," said Michael Dolle, Hale County's Agricultural Extension Agent.

Dolle estimates 40 000 ha in Hale County were affected, some severely. "The hail damage to cotton will probably result in a loss of about 40 000 bales with an estimated value of US$10 million. We estimate corn losses to be about US$2 million, and grain sorghum losses to approach $3 million."

West of Halfway one cotton producer reported baseball-size hail that fell for about 45 minutes and then dropped to pea-size. Accompanying rainfall exceeded 75 mm. Doug Nesmith, manager of the Texas Agricultural Experiment Station facility at Halfway said the producer's cotton crop was "chewed up" and only plant "stubs" remained after the storm. Nesmith and his colleagues surveyed the area west of Halfway the next morning.

"We saw pickups and cars with windshields completely broken out. Every window on the north side of buildings was broken or completely missing. And crops in field after field had been wiped out. We also saw about 15 center-pivot irrigation systems partially or completely overturned, but we are sure there were many more we did not see."

J. D. Bilbro

Large hail can demolish houses and mobile homes. Baseball-size ice falling at 170 km h^{-1} will punch holes through thin or weak roofing or cladding, and can easily crack roof tiles. Even small hail can damage crops and property (Figure 8.5). Heavy falls of small hail block drains and cause flooding, while low-pitched or flat roofs can collapse under the weight of ice. Farmers in North America respond to severe hailstorms by purchasing insurance — the only effective protection against hailstorm hazards. For instance, farmers in

Illinois in the US Midwest spend more than US$600 million annually on crop-hail insurance. When severe hailstorms are expected, the best advice is to take shelter in a substantial building.

Figure 8.5 Damage to crops caused by a hailstorm in North Dakota

National Geographic/Getty Images

Dallas–Fort Worth hailstorms, north Texas, 2003

On 5 April 2003, north Texas was hit by severe hailstorms. The hailstorms, which were accompanied by damaging winds and tornadoes, resulted in the sixth most costly natural disaster in the history of Texas.

The 2003 storms comprised three supercells, which developed along a stationary east–west front close to the New Mexico–Texas border. North of the front, surface winds were cool and from an easterly directly. Warmer, moister air, flowing from the southeast, occupied the area south of the front. At higher levels, conditions favoured the formation of supercells, with cold dry air at 500 mb altitude and a strong westerly jet stream.

The first supercell developed in the evening of 5 April at about 17.30, and was followed by the formation of a second (00.00) and third supercell (02.00). The storms moved east across the state, creating a hail **swathe** (track) that extended from Kent County in the west to Hopkins County in the east — a distance of more than 600 km. Large hailstones of up to 10 cm in diameter were reported over much of north Texas, along with several tornadoes.

In places, the hail-formed drifts were up to 2 m deep. The first supercell eventually merged with the second at 05.00, before dissipating at 07.00. The third cell dissipated at 09.00 (Figure 8.6).

Figure 8.6   Radar image of three supercells north of Dallas and Fort Worth travelling eastwards at 02.45, 6 April 2003

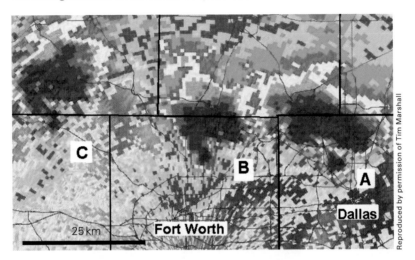

The hailstorms caused damage worth nearly US$1 billion. In Hunt County, hail destroyed several thousand hectares of wheat. Numerous roofs, gutters, windows, aeroplanes, cars and trees were damaged and at least three people were injured by large hailstones. Damage to asphalt and wood roof coverings was widespread, especially in areas where hailstones exceeded 4 cm. The number of insurance claims for roof damage increased in proportion to the size of the hailstones reported. Homes with impact-resistant roofs suffered relatively little damage. Homeowners in the area who make their properties less vulnerable to hailstorms in this way are able to claim discounts on their house insurance.

Activity 2

(a) For how long did the three supercells survive? How does this compare with a normal thunderstorm?

(b) From the evidence of Figure 8.6, what was (i) the approximate diameter of each supercell; (ii) the diameter of the storm when supercells A and B merged?

(c) Suggest reasons why the options to mitigate society's vulnerability to hailstorm hazards are so limited.

Tornado hazards

Tornadoes are nature's most violent storms; they develop in association with supercells and severe thunderstorms. Although they occur on all continents except Antarctica, tornadoes are mainly found in continental interiors in mid-latitudes, between 20° and 60°. In the USA, and especially in the Midwest and southern states, tornadoes are a major natural hazard. On average in the USA they kill between 60 and 80 people a year, injure 1500 (most deaths and injuries are due to flying debris) and cause millions of dollars of damage (Figure 8.7). In 1925, tornadoes in Missouri, Illinois and Indiana killed 695 people, and a single outbreak at Topeka (Kansas) in 1966 caused damage estimated at US$1.6 billion.

| Figure 8.7 | Tornado damage in Tennessee |

FEMA

Tornado outbreak in the US Midwest: 4 May 2003

On 4 May 2003, a massive outbreak of tornadoes developed across parts of the US Midwest and south. There were 84 reports of tornadoes, 89 of wind damage and 275 of hail. Missouri, Kansas, Tennessee and Arkansas were the worst affected, though the storms also impacted Nebraska, Oklahoma and Mississippi (Figure 8.8 and see also Table 8.2).

Figure 8.8 Storm track across the US Midwest

Tornadoes are common in the spring and autumn in the Midwest, when warm, moist air from the Gulf of Mexico collides with cold dry air from the Rockies. In fact so frequent are tornadoes in this region that the area has been dubbed 'tornado alley'. This situation, together with a powerful jet stream producing low pressure at high level, prevailed on 4 May and spawned three supercells.

The supercells, accompanied by tornadoes and hailstorms, tracked eastwards from Kansas to Tennessee. At Leavenworth County in Kansas, a deadly F4 tornado touched down at 15.55 and stayed on the ground for 1½ hours, causing one death and forcing the closure of Kansas City International Airport. Forty-five minutes later, an F3 tornado hit southeast Kansas, cutting a path nearly a kilometre wide, causing six deaths and leaving a trail of destruction in three counties.

Across the border in western Missouri, 25 tornadoes were recorded in the next few hours, ranging from category F0 to F3 (see Table 6.1 on page 54). Pierce City suffered an F3 tornado and was the scene of ten fatalities. Many occurred in a National Guard armoury where some residents had sheltered. Severe storm damage was reported in 16 counties, with fatalities in Barton, Christian, Jasper and Cedar counties. In Stockton the courthouse sustained major damage and in Battlefield the fire station was destroyed. In Dallas county, ten people were injured, several homes destroyed and the power lines brought down. Altogether, the storms accounted for 18 deaths in Missouri.

The trail of destruction continued eastwards into western Tennessee where 14 people were killed, including 11 in Jackson when an F4 tornado moved through the downtown area. The tornado also caused extensive damage to the city's fairgrounds, post office, law enforcement complex, mobile homes and hundreds of buildings.

Table 8.2 Fujita categories for the tornadoes of 4 May 2003 in Kansas, Missouri and Tennessee

Category	F0	F1	F2	F3	F4	F5	Total
Number of tornadoes	32	29	13	8	4	0	86

Mitigating the impact of tornadoes

The tornado outbreak of 3 May 2003 had been forecast by the meteorological services. In total, 186 tornado warnings and 446 severe thunderstorm warnings were issued to the emergency services, the media and the public. These warnings helped to save lives and minimised serious injuries. However, little could be done to mitigate storm damage to buildings and infrastructure. In Kansas City, local forecasters stated that 'to have such a large tornado on the ground for more than an hour in an urban area with so few injuries was a credit to everyone'.

Tornado warnings in the USA

Advance warnings of severe and dangerous weather, including tornadoes, are issued by the Storm Prediction Center (SPC). The SPC uses advanced technology to provide tornado forecasts, watches and warnings to weather forecasters, emergency managers and the aviation industry.

There are two stages of alert: a tornado watch and a tornado warning.

- A **tornado watch** defines an area where a tornado and other kinds of severe weather are possible in the next few hours. People need to be alert and be prepared to move to safe shelter if needed.
- A **tornado warning** occurs when a tornado has been spotted or when a severe thunderstorm that could spawn a tornado has been detected on Doppler radar (see Chapter 10). People are advised to take immediate precautions such as retreating to a community shelter or storm cellar. If outdoors, people should lie flat in a ditch or culvert. They should never shelter in a mobile home.

There is no doubt that advance warnings and storm shelters reduce society's vulnerability to tornados. Inadequate warnings and shelters in Bangladesh are factors that contribute to an annual death toll from tornadoes that is nearly three times higher than in the USA.

Activity 3

Investigate tornado hazards in the UK. Consider the incidence of tornadoes, their power, geographical distribution and impact. Include a case study of a recent tornadic event, such as the tornado that hit Birmingham's suburbs in July 2005. A good place to start is the TORRO website: **www.torro.org.uk/site/index.php**

9 Depressions and related weather hazards

As we saw in Chapter 7, depressions are large, travelling storms that dominate the weather in mid-latitudes. In northwest Europe, depressions are most vigorous in autumn and winter when the polar front jet stream sinks south across the region. It is during this period that depressions are most likely to bring extreme weather and related weather hazards. In this chapter we investigate a number of natural weather hazards related to depressions, such as heavy rainfall and river floods, high winds, storm surges and storm waves, and blizzards.

Heavy rainfall and flood hazards

Cumbria, November 2009

Between 20 October and 9 December 2009, an unusually strong westerly flow dominated the UK's weather. During a 7-week period, around 20 Atlantic depressions crossed the British Isles, bringing mild, stormy and exceptionally wet conditions. In fact, November 2009 turned out to be the wettest November on record, with rainfall averaging 217.4 mm across the whole country. It was also the fifth wettest month since records began.

Rainfall was particularly heavy in northwest England, southwest Scotland and north Wales. In Cumbria, Shap recorded 642 mm of rain in November, and Seathwaite in the Lake District set new national records for rainfall in 24 hours (314 mm), 2 days, 3 days, 5 days, 6 days and a week. In total, more than 1000 mm of rain were thought to have fallen

| Table 9.1 | Rainfall at Seathwaite, Cumbria: 16–20 November | |

09.00–09.00	mm	
Mon 16 November	38.6	
Tues 17 November	60.7	
Wed 18 November	142.5	
Thurs 19 November	246.6	
Total 16–19 November	**488.4**	
20.00 Wed 18– 06.00 Fri 20 November	377.7	
Peak 24-hr rainfall	316.5	New record

at Seathwaite in that month alone, with 378 mm in 34 hours between 18 and 20 November. Estimates by the Met Office suggest that these extraordinary rainfall amounts were a once-in-a-thousand-years event.

Such extreme rainfall was the result of a combination of events. First, a trailing cold front, following a southwest-to-northeast trajectory, remained more or less stationary over Cumbria and southern Scotland for 36 hours on 19 and 20 November. Second, rainfall was intensified by the orographic effect of the hills forcing the air aloft and triggering instability. Third, warm surface waters in the north Atlantic encouraged rapid evaporation and loaded the air with moisture. The hills then effectively 'squeezed' the moisture from the air. By comparison with the Lake District, surrounding lowlands in Lancashire and east Cumbria received relatively moderate amounts of rain. Morecambe, for instance, recorded only 9.5 mm on 19 November.

The causes of flooding

The extreme rainfall in November 2009, and especially on 19 and 20 November, led to widespread river flooding in Cumbria (Figure 9.1). By 20 November, six severe flood warnings were in force across the county. The River Eden burst its banks at Appleby-in-Westmorland, the River Eamont flooded at Eamont Bridge and there were floods on the River Kent at Burneside and the River Greta at Keswick (Figure 9.2). However, west Cumbria, and in particular the small market town of Cockermouth, were hardest hit.

Figure 9.1 Flooding in Cockermouth, November 2009

Global Warming Images/Alamy

Figure 9.2 | Location of the areas affected by river flooding in Cumbria

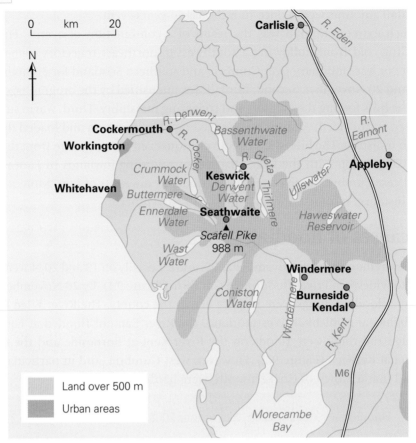

Although the primary cause of flooding was extreme rainfall in the Lakeland hills, several other factors associated with the nature of river catchments in central Lakeland played a part:

- Rapid runoff due to steep slopes, impermeable volcanic and slaty rocks (with equally impermeable boulder clay in the valleys) and relatively sparse vegetation cover: the outcome was short lag-times and high peak flows.
- High antecedent soil moisture: prior to the extreme rainfall on 19 and 20 November, the catchments had already been saturated by 4 weeks of heavy rain.
- Torrential rainfall before 19 November had filled Bassenthwaite Water, Buttermere, Crummock Water and Derwent Water — lakes all drained by the rivers Derwent and Cocker. For much of the year, the lakes normally regulate river flow and reduce extremes. Because the lakes were already full, they were unable to moderate peak flows on outlet rivers.

Flood impact

At Cockermouth, the town's flood defences were overwhelmed by the volume of water coming down the Derwent and Cocker rivers. Five hundred properties were flooded and water in the high street reached a depth of 2.5 m, causing extensive damage. More than 50 residents were rescued by RAF helicopters, and the emergency services, including firefighters, the RNLI and Mountain Rescue, were mobilised. Two hundred people were temporarily housed in reception centres in the town.

Across the county, 1300 properties were flooded and six bridges collapsed. Another 1200 were closed for safety inspections, seriously disrupting road transport. Several major roads were closed due to flooding and landslips, among them the A66, A6, A591 and A592, and people were advised to avoid all but essential travel. The collapse of the Northside Bridge (Figure 9.3) at Workington resulted in the death of a policeman. It also separated communities on opposite sides of the River Derwent, disrupting transport and life in the town, and cutting gas supplies.

| Figure 9.3 | The collapsed Northside Bridge on the River Derwent at Workington |

TopFoto

Cumbrian farmers were also badly affected by the floods. Hundreds of hectares of meadow needed for winter fodder and spring lambing were covered by thick layers of silt and gravel. The destruction of the bridge at

Lorton meant that one local farmer had to undertake a 30 km detour every day to feed his cattle. The sale of cattle and lambs at Cockermouth livestock centre was cancelled, affecting farmers' cash flows, while some farmers lost large numbers of sheep drowned in the floods.

In spite of the severity of the flooding, the overall damage and insured losses were estimated at a relatively modest £100 million. This is mainly because the area worst affected is sparsely populated. For comparison, the 2007 floods, which mainly affected South Yorkshire, Humberside and Gloucestershire, caused damage costing £2–3 billion.

Flood history and flood mitigation

Cockermouth has a long history of flooding. This is explained by its site at the confluence of the Derwent and Cocker rivers. Both rivers drain the central Lake District and, in winter, when lake levels are high, have flashy regimes with short lag-times and extreme peak flows. The flood risk increases significantly when the smaller River Cocker backs up on entering the swollen River Derwent. This happened in the 2009 floods when the River Cocker overtopped its banks and flooded the centre of Cockermouth.

Cockermouth was also flooded in 1999 and in January 2005. Following the 1999 floods, flood defences were improved with the construction of new flood embankments, floodwalls and a floodgate on the River Cocker at a cost of £600 000. A further £100 000 was spent on flood defences after the 2005 floods. These defences were designed to give protection against a once-in-a-hundred-years flood event. Local residents were also leafleted by the Environment Agency to promote flood awareness and self-help. The leaflet outlined the improved flood defences and gave advice to residents on how best to protect their properties against flooding. In 2008, the Environment Agency undertook further improvements, removing sediment from the Derwent and clearing debris from the channels of the Derwent and the Cocker.

During the 2005 floods, peak discharge reached 294 cumecs on the Derwent and 87 cumecs on the Cocker. However, official estimates of the 2009 flood by the Hazard Research Centre suggest a flood of almost biblical proportions: based on the height of the floodwater in Cockermouth, peak flow on the River Cocker was estimated have reached 255 cumecs — this from a catchment area that is barely 120 km^2. To put this in context, the highest average daily flow on the River Thames at Kingston for the whole of 2006 was 249 cumecs — and the Thames upstream from Kingston drains an area of nearly 10 000 km^2!

Storm surge and gale-force wind hazards

Depressions accompanied by gale-force winds and high tides pose major flood hazards in low-lying coastal areas. Flooding results either from the breaching of sea defences by elevated sea levels known as **storm surges** or their overtopping by storm waves. England's east coast between the Humber estuary and Kent is particularly exposed to storm surges. In 1953, a disastrous surge killed 307 people and caused widespread damage to property and infrastructure (see below and overleaf).

Storm surge in eastern England, November 2007

A more recent surge event occurred in November 2007, when a deep area of low pressure, accompanied by gale-force winds, crossed the North Sea. Northerly winds pushed water south towards the narrower and shallower parts of the North Sea basin. This situation, combined with low pressure and exceptional high tides, created a storm surge.

On 9 November, the Met Office forecast that some eastern coastal areas could face a 3 m rise in sea level — the biggest storm surge since the 1953 disaster and a direct threat to 10 000 homes. The Environment Agency (EA) warned of 'extreme danger to life and property' and placed the entire coastline from north of the Humber to Kent on flood alert (Figure 9.4). Eight severe flood warnings, 12 flood warnings and 24 flood watches were issued; the Thames Barrier was closed; and thousands of people prepared to evacuate their homes.

Figure 9.4	Environment Agency flood alerts for east coast areas, November 2007

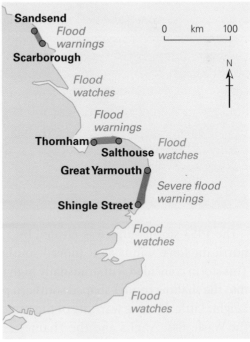

The tidal peak passed without major incident, although there was some localised flooding. Sea level rose to just 10 cm below the top of the sea walls at Great Yarmouth and, according to the EA, the sea was within a 'hair's breadth' of breaching defences elsewhere.

North Sea storm surge disaster, 1953

On 31 January and 1 February 1953, eastern England and the southern Netherlands were hit by the greatest North Sea storm surge on record. Surge heights reached 3 m at Kings Lynn and 3.36 m in the Netherlands. Dykes and flood embankments were breached and sea walls crumbled. In east and southeast England, 307 people died, 75 000 ha of farmland were flooded, and 24 000 homes damaged. The surge had even more devastating impacts in the Netherlands, where 50 dykes collapsed, 1835 people drowned and 135 000 ha of farmland were under water (Figure 9.5).

| Figure 9.5 | Storm surge impacts in the Netherlands, 1953 |

The National Archives

The 1953 storm surge was created by a deep depression, which generated hurricane-force winds as it moved southeastwards through the North Sea. This storm coincided with unusually high tides. As the surge moved south and into the shallow funnel-shaped southern part of the North Sea, it increased in height. Little advance warning of the surge was given to communities around the Wash, East Anglia and the Thames estuary because telephone lines had been brought down further north in Lincolnshire by the severity of the storm.

Responses

Following the floods, the UK government set up a committee to consider, among other things, the status of the country's east coast sea defences and improvements to flood warnings. Eventually this led to the development of a Storm Tide Forecasting Service (STFS). In 2006–07, the STFS issued 201 alerts for the east coast, including 125 surge events. A decision was also taken to strengthen and raise hard sea defences to the level of the 1953 floods in areas of high property value and agricultural importance. Ultimately the 1953 flooding highlighted the serious flood risk to London and the Thames estuary. This resulted in the construction of the Thames Barrier some 30 years later.

In the Netherlands, the long-term response to the 1953 storm surge disaster was a massive engineering project to seal off the Rhine–Maas delta, and protect those areas at greatest risk. The so-called Delta Project involved the construction of ten dams and two bridges and reduced the length of the coastline from 800 km to 80 km. Engineering work was only completed in the mid-1980s with the closure of the Eastern Scheldt estuary. The final cost of the project was US$5 billion.

Activity 1

Log on to **en.wikipedia.org/wiki/Delta_Works**

(a) Read the web pages and study the map of the Delta Project. Explain how the length of the coastline in the Rhine–Maas delta was reduced.

(b) Explain why the Eastern Scheldt was protected by a storm surge barrier rather than a dam.

(c) In addition to flood control, suggest other possible benefits of the project for the Rhine–Maas delta region.

Gale-force winds and storm waves, October 2004

On 27 and 28 October 2004, the coincidence of spring tides and a deep depression with gusts of 120 km h^{-1} generated waves as high as four-storey buildings and caused the worst coastal flooding in Cornwall and Devon for 30 years. At Penzance in Cornwall, waves overtopped sea defences, flooding properties in the surrounding streets and the main railway line. Further along the coast at Flushing, at high tide the main street and 40 houses were knee-deep in water. At Looe, waves broke over the sea wall and people were evacuated from their homes into the church hall. In Devon, the seafronts at Torquay, Sidmouth, Paignton and Exmouth were closed because of high waves and flying debris; beach huts were torn to shreds at Dawlish and sea walls were damaged. Torbay Council estimated the final repair bill at £1 million. Train services were severely disrupted following the breakdown of two trains after waves swamped the coastal line between Teignmouth and Dawlish. More than 100 people had to be rescued from the stranded trains. Across the southwest, thousands of trees were blown down. Meanwhile, the floods forced the closure of many roads, bringing the southern parts of the county to a virtual standstill.

Activity 2

With reference to the UK, investigate how and why climate change is likely to affect (a) the frequency and power of depressions; (b) the incidence of extreme weather such as heavy rainfall and related floods, high winds, storm surges and coastal floods. Search official government and newspaper websites online, for example the Met Office, the Environment Agency, the Centre for Ecology and Hydrology, the Treasury, the *Guardian* and the *Daily Telegraph*.

Heavy snowfall and blizzard hazards

Blizzards develop when heavy snowfall is driven by strong winds. Such extreme weather is most often caused by deep depressions and frontal systems during spells of sub-zero temperatures. Blizzards disrupt all forms of transport. For example, in the UK in mid-December 2009, heavy snowfalls halted high-speed rail services through the Channel Tunnel for 3 days and closed several international airports (see Chapter 11). However, the impact of heavy snowfall and blizzards depends not just on the severity of the weather, but also on levels of preparedness. In much of England, where on average snow lies on the ground for fewer than half-a-dozen days each winter, even a light fall can be highly disruptive. In contrast, in Scandinavia, where there is a prolonged snow cover every winter, levels of preparedness are high and disruption is on a much smaller scale.

Snow and blizzards in the northeast USA, 19–20 December 2009

A powerful depression, which originated over the Gulf of Mexico, hit the northeast USA on 19 and 20 December 2009. Further south, the storm had caused flash floods but as it tracked northeast it met cold air over the northern states and the rain turned to snow. Heavy snow and strong winds created blizzard and white-out conditions in Long Island and southern New England. Snowfalls of 25–50 cm were widespread. New York City recorded 64 cm — its heaviest snowfall for 3 years. Washington DC, with 40 cm, had its biggest-ever snowfall for a December day (Figure 9.6).

Figure 9.6 Northeast USA

The blizzard created havoc, bringing traffic to a standstill, downing power lines and causing five storm-related fatalities. Even by 21 December, blizzard warnings remained in force for parts of Rhode Island and Massachusetts, where winds gusted up to 90 km h^{-1}. In Virginia, three people died: one was killed when a car hit a tree; a second died of exposure; and a third was involved in a road traffic accident. In Ohio, two people were killed in accidents on snow-covered roads.

Transport disruption was widespread. Airports at Washington and Philadelphia closed; there were long delays at Baltimore; and many flights from New York and Philadelphia were cancelled. Delays on Amtrak averaged 30 minutes to 1 hour on Washington–Boston services and two trains were delayed by 4 hours. Near Farmingdale on Long Island, about 150 people were stranded on a train for more than 5 hours by a combination of snow drifts, icing, traffic problems and equipment failures caused by the severe weather.

Mitigating responses to heavy snowfalls and blizzards

Responses to extreme winter weather conditions in North America and Europe, involving heavy snow and blizzards, are shown in Table 9.2.

Table 9.2 Mitigating responses to snowfall and blizzards in North America and Europe

Early warning	In the UK, the Met Office issues severe weather warnings for snow; similar warnings are issued in the USA by the National Weather Center
Gritting road surfaces	In the UK, local authorities keep stockpiles of rock salt and fleets of gritting lorries to keep roads clear of snow
Snow clearance	Snowploughs and snow blowers are used on roads and airport runways
Drift reduction	On exposed roads, especially at high level, snow fences help to reduce the drifting across road surfaces
De-icing	Removal of ice, which builds up on power lines or on aircraft wings; methods may involve mechanical (heat) or chemical (spray) processes

0 Tropical cyclone hazards

Tropical cyclones are responsible for a number of related natural hazards, such as damaging high winds; storm surges and coastal flooding; heavy rain; and river flooding and landslips.

Related hazards

High winds

Sustained winds can reach 250 km h^{-1} in the cyclone wall around the eye, with gusts up to 360 km h^{-1}. Destruction results from both direct impact and flying debris. Wind speed is a primary cause of damage to trees and crops: entire forests can be flattened by hurricane-force winds. Tall buildings are also vulnerable to collapse. Sudden pressure change can cause buildings to implode, while suction can lift up roofs and entire buildings. However, most destruction, death and injury are caused by debris. Poorly fastened roof sheets, tiles, telephone poles and other building parts are the most common projectiles.

Storm surges

Storm surges present major hazards along low-lying coasts with shallow continental shelves, such as the Gulf of Mexico. An advancing surge combined with high tides can raise local sea levels by as much as 8 m. Meanwhile, low atmospheric pressure also pushes up the sea surface. The resulting rise in water level can breach or overtop sea defences and lead to flooding, damage to property and loss of life.

Intense rainfall

Rains accompanying tropical cyclones are often torrential and may last for several days. Local topography, humidity and the forward speed of a tropical cyclone are important factors influencing rainfall amounts.
  Intense rainfall causes three types of hazard:
- water seepage into buildings, resulting in their collapse from the weight of the absorbed water

- inland flooding by swollen rivers
- mass movements on slopes, such as landslides, mudslides, mudflows and debris flows: heavy rain lubricates slope materials, reduces their coherence and frictional resistance to gravity, and triggers downslope movement

Flooding and mass movement hazards related to Hurricane Mitch

Between 28 September and 2 October 1998, the slow-moving Hurricane Mitch dumped nearly 500 mm of rain a day on the uplands of Honduras and Nicaragua. In northwest Honduras, the rains turned the Ulúa and Chamelecón rivers into vast lakes, and ruined most of the nation's banana crop (Figure 10.1)

| Figure 10.1 | Honduras and surrounding countries |

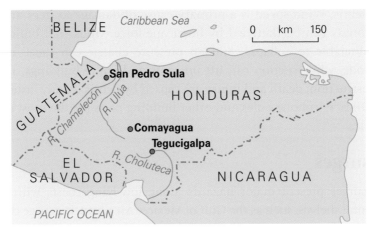

Refugees, sheltering in tented camps, were swept away. In the Honduran capital, Tegucigalpa, the floods rose two storeys high, drowning people who had climbed onto rooftops. In the northern mountains of Nicaragua, flood-waters cut deep ravines in hillsides and destroyed a third of the country's cash crops. Many who survived the floods died later from disease. Other survivors in the most isolated areas faced starvation.

Mass movement hazards

Torrential rain triggered several hundred mass movement events within the cities of Tegucigalpa and Comayagua and the surrounding countryside. Most of these were fast-moving debris flows with run-out distances of several hundred metres. A major landslide below the summit of Cerro El Berrinche in Tegucigalpa destroyed the slum settlement of Soto and parts of several neighbouring slums. The slide also dammed the Río Choluteca, creating a barrier lake of stagnant, sewage-filled water, which presented a major health risk.

Responding to tropical cyclone hazards

Tropical cyclones are more closely monitored than any other natural hazard. In MEDCs, detailed measurements of temperature, humidity, wind speed and storm paths are obtained from satellites, aircraft, ships and buoys. Increasingly these methods are being used to mitigate the effects of tropical cyclone hazards in poorer countries like Bangladesh and India. In the USA, accurate forecasts, updates and warnings are issued by agencies such as the US National Weather Service and the National Hurricane Center.

Storm surges are the most deadly hazard accompanying tropical cyclones. On the Gulf coast of the USA, major cities such as New Orleans, Houston and Galveston are protected by flood embankments or **levées** (Figure 10.2). In Bangladesh and India, thousands of lives have been saved by storm shelters, built on stilts, which provide temporary refuge during storm surges. Where storms are closely monitored, early warning may invoke mass evacuations such as those in New Orleans in 2005 (Hurricane Katrina) and in Houston in 2008 (Hurricane Ike; see Figure 10.3 on page 101).

| Figure 10.2 | A levée on the Mississippi

Infrogmation

In the USA, people living in areas exposed to hurricanes are encouraged to take responsibility for themselves and their families. The National Oceanic and Atmospheric Administration (NOAA) has a hurricane preparedness website that gives advice on matters such as locating safe areas, escape routes, insurance cover, emergency supplies and so on.

The USA also has the government-sponsored Federal Emergency Management Agency (FEMA), whose mission includes responding to, aiding recovery from, and helping to mitigate natural disasters. Within 3 months of the Hurricane Ike disaster in September 2008, FEMA had opened 128 disaster recovery centres in Texas serving 128 000 people. It had also provided temporary shelter and accommodation in hotels and motels for 26 500 families. Six months after the disaster, FEMA had provided US$519 million in disaster assistance for housing and other disaster-related needs, and committed a further US$600 million.

Measuring and monitoring tropical cyclones

Monitoring begins out in the ocean in the early stages of storm development. At this stage only indirect measurements are possible, using satellites, ships and buoys moored at sea. Closer to land, direct measurements are made by aircraft, radiosondes and dropsondes. Data are fed into computer models that forecast storm intensities and tracks.

Specific sources of information available to weather forecasters include the following:

- **Geostationary satellites** provide data on the size, intensity and movement of storms (Figure 10.3).
- **Ships and buoys** record air temperature, sea-surface temperature, wind speed, wind direction, pressure and humidity.
- **Aircraft** flying into the storms measure wind speed, air pressure, temperature and humidity.
- **Radiosondes and dropsondes** — small instrument packages and radio transmitters attached to balloons and released into storms or dropped from aircraft — provide additional information on temperature, wind speed, pressure and humidity.
- **Doppler radar** provides radar images of rainfall intensity.

The US National Weather Center issues two categories of warning of approaching hurricanes:

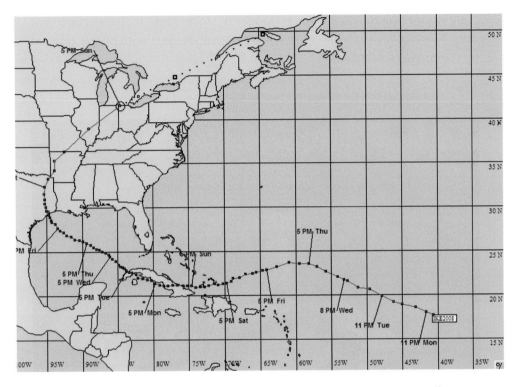

Figure 10.3 National Hurricane Center map showing the track followed by Hurricane Ike across the Caribbean and Gulf of Mexico in 2008

- **Hurricane watch**: announcements are made for specific coastal areas that hurricane conditions are possible within the next 36 hours.
- **Hurricane warning**: announcements for specific coastal areas that sustained winds of 119 km h^{-1} and above are expected in the next 24 hours.

Hurricane Katrina

Hurricane Katrina slammed into the Gulf coast of Louisiana at 06.10 on 29 August 2005 (Figure 10.4). Although by the time Katrina made landfall it had weakened from a

Figure 10.4 Satellite image of Hurricane Katrina

category 5 to a category 4 storm, it was the third most intense hurricane to make landfall in the USA. Katrina's impact was catastrophic. The storm killed 1353 people and 270 000 homes were either damaged or destroyed (Figure 10.5). Eighty per cent of New Orleans was flooded by storm surge, with water up to 6 m deep. Much of the city's lower ninth ward was submerged, with people trapped on rooftops and in attics.

Figure 10.5 Floods caused by storm surges in New Orleans

Economic losses exceeded US$100 billion. Ten thousand jobs were lost due to damage to businesses and infrastructure (e.g. major highways). Oil and gas production in the coastal waters of the Gulf was badly disrupted, with damage to 30 production platforms and the shutting down of nine oil refineries. In economic terms, Hurricane Katrina proved to be the costliest natural disaster in US history.

Exposure

The Gulf of Mexico is no stranger to hurricanes. On average every year three or four major storms batter this coast, leaving a wake of destruction in Florida, Alabama, Louisiana, Mississippi and Texas. Hurricane activity has been above average in the Atlantic region since 1995. Even so, the 2005 hurricane season broke all records. There were 15 hurricanes in the Atlantic region: five reached category 4 status, and four became category 5. In fact 2005 was the first time that more than one category 5 hurricane had developed in the Atlantic region in a single season.

At its peak, Hurricane Katrina produced sustained winds speeds of 281 km h^{-1} with gusts exceeding 344 km h^{-1}. These high winds and a central pressure of just 902 mb generated a storm surge of 8–9 m. The city of New Orleans is at high risk from storm surges because most of it lies below sea level. The Katrina storm surge reached 6 m, breaching four levées, overtopping several others and causing disastrous floods.

Adding to exposure are the 9.5 million people living in coastal counties along the Gulf of Mexico between Louisiana and Florida (Table 10.1) including several large metropolitan areas (Figure 10.6). Overall population densities in the coastal districts are more than twice the US average and rapid population growth in these areas in recent years has added to exposure levels.

Table 10.1 Population of coastal counties along the Gulf of Mexico, 2004

	Population in coastal counties	% of total state population in coastal counties
Alabama	727 090	16
Florida	6 800 000	39
Louisiana	3 555 628	79
Mississippi	667 635	21

Figure 10.6 Major metropolitan areas along the Gulf Coast

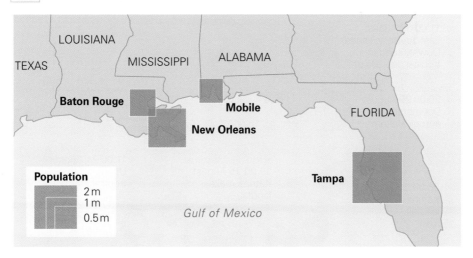

Vulnerability

Land subsidence and the loss of wetlands in the Mississippi delta
Hurricane Katrina was an extreme weather event. Yet this alone does not explain the scale of the disaster. This is because vulnerability, as well as

exposure, played a key part in Katrina's impact. Experts agree that flooding by the storm surge was made worse by the loss of wetlands in the Mississippi delta. In the past 50 years, 90 km² of wetland in the delta have disappeared. Wetlands provide a valuable flood protection service, storing surplus water and absorbing the impact of storm surges. Losses of wetland in the delta were the result of several factors: drainage for land reclamation; subsidence due to the extraction of natural gas; and slowing in rates of sedimentation and accretion. The last is arguably the most serious. It has been caused by the building of levées to protect farmland and industrial installations from flooding. But 'walling-in' the Mississippi River, together with the construction of dams upstream, has starved the delta of the silt needed to keep pace with subsidence. Many scientists are calling for the restoration of the delta's wetlands as the only sustainable solution to the threat posed by future storm surges.

Short-term mitigation

No country is better prepared to deal with tropical storm hazards than the USA. Katrina's progress was closely monitored as it intensified and Katrina was upgraded from a tropical depression on 23 August to a tropical storm on 24 August and finally to a category 5 hurricane 5 days later (Figure 10.7).

Figure 10.7 Storm track of Katrina

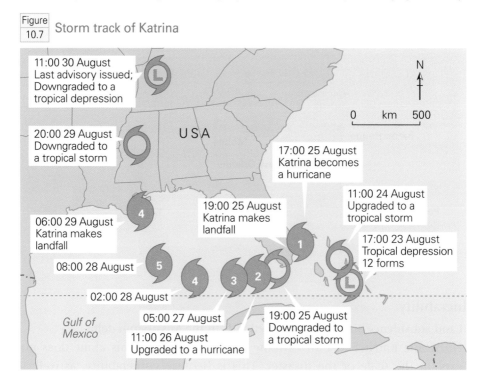

11:00 30 August
Last advisory issued;
Downgraded to a
tropical depression

20:00 29 August
Downgraded to
a tropical storm

USA

17:00 25 August
Katrina becomes
a hurricane

11:00 24 August
Upgraded to a
tropical storm

06:00 29 August
Katrina makes
landfall

19:00 25 August
Katrina makes
landfall

17:00 23 August
Tropical depression
12 forms

08:00 28 August

02:00 28 August

Gulf of
Mexico

05:00 27 August

19:00 25 August
Downgraded to
a tropical storm

11:00 26 August
Upgraded to a hurricane

N

0   km   500

Before Katrina made landfall, the National Weather Service issued hurricane watches and warnings with an 8-hour lead time. Forecasts of the location and time of landfall were accurate and assisted in one of the largest evacuations in US history.

The mayor of New Orleans ordered an evacuation of the city on 28 August. The city's Superdome sports arena and conference centre were designated 'refuges of last resort' for the 150 000 people unable to flee the city. Although these measures did little to reduce the physical and economic damage caused by the storm, 80% of the people at risk were successfully evacuated — a response that saved thousands of lives. Two days before Katrina made landfall, President George W. Bush declared a state of emergency in Alabama and Mississippi. The governor of Louisiana made a similar declaration on 26 August.

Long-term mitigation

The Hurricane Katrina storm surge that devastated New Orleans was a disaster waiting to happen (see Figure 10.8). New Orleans is, after all, a city surrounded by water: Lake Pontchartrain lies to the north and the Mississippi River to the south. Moreover, the city's site is on average is 2 m below sea

Figure 10.8 New Orleans flood map

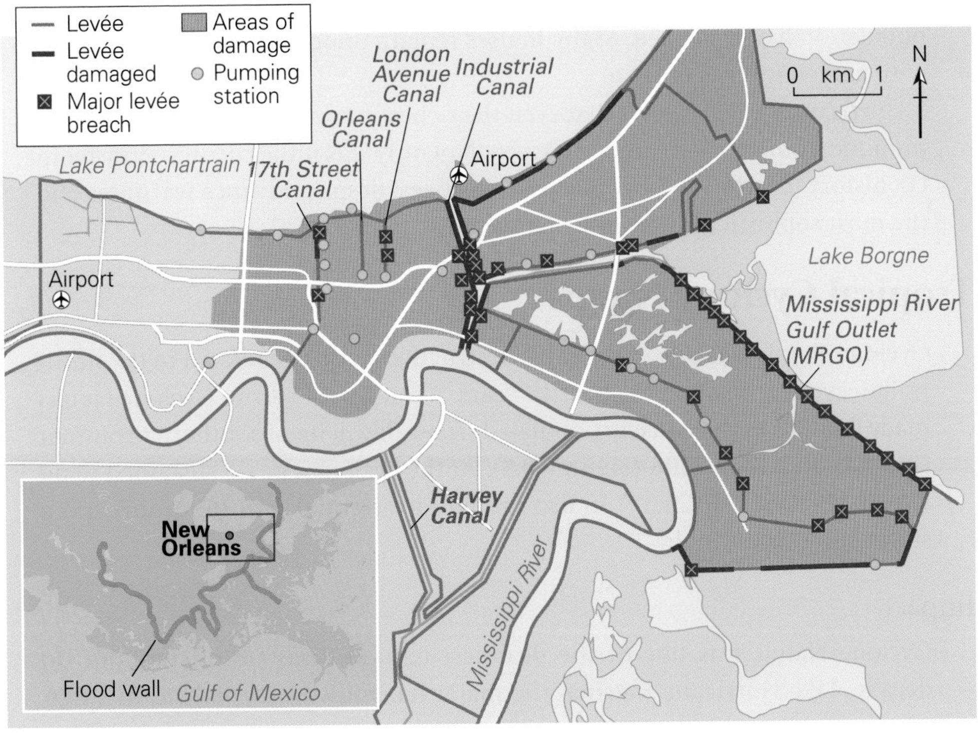

level. Without flood defences, New Orleans could not exist. Its security and survival depend on a 560 km levée system. However, this system was designed to give protection only against hurricanes up to category 3 intensity; the levées were not built for a hurricane of Katrina's intensity. The situation was made worse by the Mississippi River Gulf Outlet. This 200 metre-wide canal acted as a funnel for the storm surge, increasing its height by 20% and doubling its speed.

Despite the known risks, New Orleans' levée system had been poorly maintained and was in urgent need of strengthening. Aware of the problem, a year before the disaster the US Army Corps of Engineers asked the federal government for US$105 million to strengthen New Orleans's flood defences. It got just US$40 million.

Following the Katrina disaster, a multi-billion-dollar scheme was launched to strengthen the flood defences. By 2011 it aims to raise the levées to a height capable of withstanding a category 5 hurricane. New pumping stations are also being built to remove floodwater from the city.

Some experts question whether protecting certain areas of the city, and especially those that lie up to 2 m below sea level, is sustainable. Rising sea level and the sinking delta may eventually mean that some parts of New Orleans have to be abandoned permanently. In the lower ninth ward, one of the neighbourhoods most badly affected by the floods, less than 20% of the population have returned. Many houses remain unoccupied, boarded up and with garden lots overgrown.

Hurricane Katrina shows that even the richest countries in the world are not immune from major weather disasters. Not only was it the costliest disaster in US history, nearly 1400 people lost their lives, despite advance warnings and the most sophisticated monitoring systems.

Tropical Cyclone Nargis

Cyclone Nargis was one of the most destructive storms generated in the north Indian cyclone basin in the past 40 years. A category 4 storm, Cyclone Nargis made landfall in the densely populated Irrawaddy delta of southern Myanmar (Burma) on 2 May 2008 (Figure 10.9). At the cyclone's peak, sustained wind speeds reached 210 km h^{-1}. It also produced torrential rain (600 mm) and a storm surge 3.5 m high.

Impact

Cyclone Nargis was one of the deadliest natural disasters of the 2001–10 decade. Like Hurricane Katrina, the major hazard was a lethal storm surge,

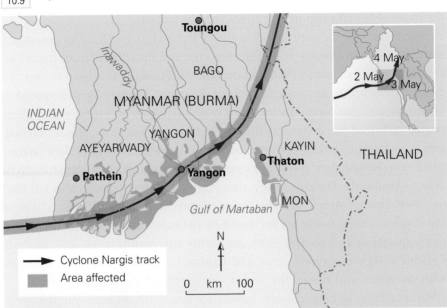

Figure
10.9
Myanmar and the track of Cyclone Nargis

which swept through the Irrawaddy delta region. The surge killed an estimated 140 000 people, destroyed 450 000 homes and damaged 350 000 others. Up to 800 000 people were made homeless. In the worst-affected areas, 85% of homes were wrecked, and in total three-quarters of health facilities and 4000 schools were ruined or badly damaged.

The cyclone also inflicted severe damage on the delta's rural economy and infrastructure. It flooded 600 000 ha of farmland, killed half the livestock, and destroyed fishing boats, food stocks and agricultural equipment. By mid-June there were serious food shortages and the area planted to rice (the staple food crop) had fallen by 25%. Following the disaster, overall rice production in Myanmar was down by 6%, raising fears of food security.

Exposure and vulnerability

Tropical cyclones and storm surges present a major threat to populations in the low-lying coastal regions around the Bay of Bengal. The scale of the Cyclone Nargis disaster underlined the extreme levels of exposure and vulnerability in southern Myanmar. Exposure is increased by some of the highest rural population densities in the world. The Irrawaddy delta supports 3.5 million people at an average density of 100 per square kilometre.

The impact of Cyclone Nargis in southern Myanmar was catastrophic. Loss of life was around 100 times greater than in the Hurricane Katrina disaster.

Although the absolute cost in economic terms was less than Katrina, the relative costs were much higher: the economy and infrastructure of much of the Irrawaddy delta region was effectively destroyed.

Explanation for the contrasting scales of the Nargis and Katrina disasters is not to be found in *exposure*: southern Myanmar and the US Gulf coast states have similar levels of exposure. What makes the difference is southern Myanmar's greater *vulnerability* to tropical cyclone hazards. Poverty is widespread in Myanmar and this single factor has a huge influence on vulnerability. Most people living in areas hardest hit by Cyclone Nargis were peasant farmers and their families living in flimsy houses. Few owned the land they farmed; some even rented their tools and draught animals; and most were heavily in debt to landlords. Poverty meant that people had few resources to fall back on when disaster struck; and, for the survivors, recovery is difficult and slow. Their vulnerability is further increased by the nature of the local economy — rice production and fishing. Both are highly susceptible to cyclone hazards. Cyclone Nargis destroyed crops and fishing boats, contaminated farmland with salt water, and ruined the livelihoods of tens of thousands of people.

Vulnerability is also closely linked to levels of disaster preparedness. Unlike neighbouring Bangladesh, where warnings of Cyclone Nargis were issued 36 hours in advance and precautions and storm shelters activated, the Myanmar government provided no warnings of the impending disaster. Moreover, levées and storm shelters, which offer some protection against storm surges, are absent in the Irrawaddy delta. Vulnerability was further increased by the degradation of coastal mangrove forests. These salt-tolerant forests, which occupy the inter-tidal zone, provide a natural buffer and protection against storm surges.

Activity 1

(a) Log on to www.globalenvision.org/2009/05/14/burmese-farmers-caught-poverty-trap

Study the video on life in Bogale township in the Irrawaddy delta in the aftermath of Cyclone Nargis.

Describe (i) the vulnerability of farmers in Bogale; (ii) the impact of Cyclone Nargis; (iii) the effect of the global economic downturn in 2008–09 on rural livelihoods.

(b) Discuss the view that a nation need not be wealthy or technologically advanced to be well prepared for tropical cyclone disasters. Use the internet to contrast approaches to disaster mitigation in the context of Cyclone Nargis in Myanmar, and Cyclone Sidr (2007) and Cyclone Aila (2009) in Bangladesh.

Responding to the disaster

Politically isolated and secretive, the Myanmar government initially responded by declining international aid and trying to manage the disaster alone. However, given the magnitude of the disaster, the government was forced to soften its stance and allow aid agencies and aid workers access to the country. Emergency aid had two objectives. The first was to provide urgent humanitarian assistance in the form of food, shelter, clean water and medical supplies. By July, 13 UN agencies and 23 NGOs were working in the disaster area. However, delays due to government obstruction and intransigence meant that by this time barely half of those affected by the disaster had received any humanitarian aid.

The second objective was to rebuild damaged infrastructure, such as roads, bridges, schools and hospitals, and restore livelihoods. Estimates of the cost of the disaster are around US$10 billion. Given the fact that Myanmar is one of the poorest countries in Asia, recovery will depend on long-term support from the international community.

In the first 3 months after the disaster, the UN's appeal for relief aid raised US$95 million. This was enough to ensure that none of the cyclone survivors died of starvation. A revised UN appeal covering the period from August 2008 to April 2009 aimed to raise nearly US$500 million. Even so, after 12 months, of the 800 000 people displaced by Cyclone Nargis, 130 000 were still living in temporary shelters and there remained an acute shortage of jobs. In the medium term, priorities are focused on rebuilding the rural economy and re-establishing economic sustainability.

Increasing frequency of hurricane activity

Many scientists believe there is a link between the frequency and intensity of hurricanes in the Atlantic Basin and global warming. Hurricanes get their energy from the oceans, and rising sea temperatures should in theory generate more frequent and more powerful storms. Moreover, in recent years, sea-surface temperatures in the Gulf of Mexico have been the highest on record; in 2005 they were 1 °C above average. Nonetheless, the hurricane seasons of 2006, 2007 and 2009 were unusually quiet, suggesting that any relationship between hurricane frequency and global warming is both complex and, as yet, poorly understood.

An even stronger relationship exists between the frequency of hurricane activity in the Atlantic Basin and the El Niño Southern Oscillation (ENSO) (see below). During **El Niño** events, when surface waters in the eastern equatorial Pacific Ocean are unusually warm, hurricane activity is low. The reverse is true in **La Niña** years, when cold surface water spreads eastwards through the equatorial Pacific. For example, in the period 1900–83, of the 54 major hurricanes that affected the US Gulf coast, only four occurred in El Niño years. The most active Atlantic hurricane season on record — 2005 — which included 15 hurricanes, of which seven were category 3 and above, was also a La Niña year.

The El Niño Southern Oscillation and weather patterns

'El Niño' and 'La Niña' are terms used to describe ocean temperature anomalies in the equatorial Pacific Ocean. These anomalies follow a cyclical pattern, every 3–9 years oscillating between warm (El Niño) and cold (La Niña) conditions. This phenomenon is known as the **El Niño Southern Oscillation** (ENSO). Between 1976 and 2009, there were nine El Niño/La Niña events.

In normal years, trade winds transport warm surface water westwards across the equatorial Pacific, and allow upwelling of cold water off the west coast of South America. However, during an El Niño event, the trade winds weaken, and a deep layer of warm water in the western Pacific spreads eastwards. The result is unusually high SSTs in central and eastern equatorial parts of the Pacific Ocean, and along the west coast of South America. The El Niño that occurred between May 2009 and spring 2010 had, by late January 2010, resulted in a 1–3 °C increase in SST in the equatorial Pacific.

Activity 2

Find out more about El Niño and La Niña by logging on to the NOAA website:
www.elnino.noaa.gov/lanina.html
(a) What are El Niño and La Niña?
(b) Describe the current El Niño/La Niña conditions in the Pacific Ocean. You can get an update at: **www.cpc.noaa.gov/products/analysis_monitoring/enso_advisory/**
(c) With reference to the El Niño Southern Oscillation (ENSO) and the North Atlantic Oscillation (NAO), explain the meaning of the term 'teleconnection'.
(d) Explain how and why El Niño and La Niña often give rise to extreme weather around the Pacific Ocean.

11 Anticyclones and weather hazards

Anticyclones are areas of high pressure associated with stable and calm conditions. However, they are just as likely to give rise to extreme weather events than low-pressure areas such as depressions and tropical cyclones. Whereas low-pressure areas can bring intense but short-lived extremes, anticyclonic conditions tend to be prolonged and may last for several weeks or even months. Among the extreme events are droughts, heatwaves and cold spells. Related hazards include dust storms and wildfires.

Drought

Droughts are prolonged periods of weather with abnormally low rainfall, and can be defined in meteorological, agricultural and hydrological terms (Table 11.1). They are gradual phenomena, which ultimately lead to water shortages. The impact of drought is felt first in activities that are most dependent on rainfall, such as crop growing, ranching, river transport and power supply. Severe droughts may threaten public water supplies and also result in low river flow, with damaging effects on aquatic life.

Table 11.1 Definitions of drought

Meteorological drought	Meteorological drought occurs when there is a prolonged period with less than average precipitation. It has a direct impact on agriculture and water supplies
Agricultural drought	Agricultural drought is a prolonged shortfall in soil moisture, which reduces crop yields and the productivity of pastureland. Agriculture is usually the first economic activity to be affected by drought
Hydrological drought	Hydrological drought occurs when the water reserves in aquifers, snowpacks, lakes and reservoirs fall significantly below the seasonal average. It may be influenced by factors other than rainfall, e.g. land-use change, land degradation

Causes of drought

The main meteorological cause of drought is persistent high pressure. This blocks the passage of low-pressure systems that normally bring precipitation. Blocking (see Chapter 7) occurs in western Europe when high pressure builds over the continent, deflecting weather systems either north or south of their normal storm track. The result is below average rainfall. If this situation lasts for several weeks, especially in spring or summer, it can create drought conditions. The droughts in the UK in summer 1976 and autumn 1995 were the result of such anticyclonic blocking.

Droughts also occur in the tropics and subtropics when seasonal rains fail and high pressure prevails. In south Asia, the failure of the monsoon rains in 2009 led to drought and food shortages. Similar events have occurred in sub-Saharan Africa in the past two decades when seasonal rains have failed to materialise and droughts have occurred on an epic scale. Drought conditions were especially severe in northern Kenya, Ethiopia, Somalia and Uganda in 2009, causing crop failure, killing domestic livestock and wildlife, and threatening the livelihoods of over 20 million people. Droughts in monsoon Asia and sub-Saharan Africa are increasingly linked to global climate change and desertification, the latter caused in part by deforestation, overgrazing, overcultivation and population growth.

Drought in California, 2007–09

California experienced three successive years of drought from 2007 to 2009. The drought had severe impacts on California's economy, while water shortages, together with high summer temperatures and strong winds, caused devastating wildfires.

Meteorological causes of drought

Most of California has a Mediterranean-type climate with mild wet winters and warm dry summers (Table 11.2). High pressure dominates the summer months. In autumn, the high pressure shifts south, allowing depressions and moist air to invade from the Pacific. Thus, on average, 86% of California's annual rainfall comes between November and March, and nearly half falls in the 3 months from December to February.

Following 2 years of drought, January 2009 proved exceptionally dry (Table 11.2) with rainfall just one-third of the average. Because January is normally the wettest month, it has a critical influence on California's water supplies. The failure of the January 2009 rains was due to the persistence of a strong blocking anticyclone over the southwest USA and the north Pacific

Ocean. The anticyclone pushed the jet stream and Pacific storms north of their usual track, bringing heavy rains to the northwest USA but leaving California unusually dry.

Scientists believe that this winter weather pattern, which prevailed for much of the period 2007–09, is connected to sea-surface temperatures (SSTs) in the equatorial Pacific Ocean. During a La Niña phase, when SSTs are significantly lower than average, drought conditions develop in the US southwest (Figure 11.1). In El Niño years, when surface waters in the equatorial Pacific Ocean are unusually warm, teleconnections (see Chapter 10 and below) with the US southwest tend to result in periods of above-average rainfall and widespread flooding.

Table 11.2	California rainfall, 2008–09		
Month	**Mean (mm)**	**Actual (mm)**	**% mean**
October	31	19	61
November	71	63	89
December	99	77	78
January	110	32	29
February	93	129	139
March	79	54	68
April	42	15	36
May	23	38	165
June	9	12	133
July	5	1	20
August	7	2	29
September	12	2	17

Figure 11.1 Low water levels on Lake Powell, southwest USA, following several years of drought

Michael Raw

The El Niño Southern Oscillation and drought

Because the Pacific Ocean covers nearly half the surface area of the planet, the **coupling** between the atmosphere and the ocean surface has a profound impact on weather events around the world. In El Niño years, this **teleconnection** brings drought conditions to Australia, southeast Asia and eastern Brazil, with forest and bush fires. Meanwhile, enhanced evaporation from the warm ocean in the eastern Pacific causes torrential rain and flooding in Peru and the southern USA.

La Niña is a reverse situation, when an unusually cold tongue of water, covering millions of square kilometres, occupies the equatorial Pacific. It produces opposite weather impacts to El Niño.

During El Niño years there is a reduction in tropical cyclone activity in the Atlantic, Caribbean, Gulf of Mexico and western Pacific. In contrast, La Niña is associated with more frequent tropical cyclones in these regions.

Impact of drought

The 2007–09 drought had major economic impacts on agriculture, a leading economic sector in California. The state produces half of all fresh fruit and vegetables consumed in the USA and Canada, and is also a major producer of dairy products, olives and nuts. By 2009, water allocations to agriculture for irrigation in the western Central Valley had been cut to just 10% of normal (cuts in 2007 and 2008 were 40% and 50% respectively) and, at the start of the year, water storage in surface reservoirs was only 65% of normal. Soil moisture deficits meant that many farmers had to leave arable land fallow, and avocado and citrus growers were forced to cut down trees because of insufficient irrigation water and big increases in water charges. Total agricultural losses for 2009 were expected to reach US$3 billion. Rural counties most dependent on agriculture experienced high levels of unemployment — up to 40% in some places — and, among poorer groups, there were reports of food shortages and homelessness.

Meanwhile hydroelectric power (HEP) generation, fisheries and wildlife, and recreation were also badly affected. In 2008, low water levels in rivers and reservoirs reduced the proportion of electrical energy generated by HEP in California to just 8%, compared to 16.6% in 2006. Low river levels were also responsible for fish kills and disruptions to the migration of Pacific salmon. Localised effects of the drought on recreation included a lack of snow in the Sierra Nevada mountains affecting ski resorts, and low water elevations in reservoirs and rivers limiting activities such as sailing and rafting.

Response

In February 2009 the drought was sufficiently critical for the Governor of California to proclaim a state of emergency. Among the emergency measures were: an instruction that all urban water users should reduce consumption by 20%; arrangements to speed up the transfer of water from suppliers to consumers; technical assistance to farmers to promote more efficient use of water; and a state-wise campaign to encourage water conservation. Individual counties introduced their own mandatory regulations. For example, in San Diego, restrictions were placed on garden watering, irrigation sprinklers, vehicle washing and overfilling swimming pools. It was also mandatory to repair leaks within 72 hours.

The US Department of Agriculture (USDA) responded by providing disaster assistance for drought-hit Californian farmers. A federal drought action team for California was set up in February 2009, and by May farmers in 48 of California's 58 counties were eligible for financial support for losses due to the drought.

Exposure and vulnerability

California suffers high exposure to drought hazards. Mean annual rainfall is relatively low, and water supplies depend crucially on the amount of rain falling between December and February. The low rainfall in January 2009 was enough to ensure that California's drought continued for a third year. Adding to exposure is the huge demand for water. This is partly due to the size of California's population (37 million) and also to high standards of living, which drive up per capita water consumption. For example, water consumption averages 850 litres per person per day in Los Angeles, while in rural Merced County in the Central Valley per capita consumption reaches 1375 litres a day.

Drought risk is also affected by vulnerability. California's economic dependence on agriculture makes it especially vulnerable to drought hazards. California has the largest agricultural economy of any state in the USA, and an estimated one in six jobs are tied to agriculture in some way. Few economic activities are more sensitive to drought than agriculture and this is a particular concern in counties like Fresno, where agriculture is by far the leading economic activity.

On the other hand, California's drought vulnerability is reduced by the state's elaborate water infrastructure. Water resources are managed by an extensive system of surface reservoirs, boreholes and aqueducts. Aqueducts transfer water from the Owens Valley in eastern California to Los Angeles, and from Lake Havasu on the Colorado River to southern California. One-third of California's water comes from the Sierra Nevada mountains. There the snowpack that forms each winter provides a natural water store. Snowmelt in the spring and summer releases water during the dry summer months and compensates for the virtual absence of rain between May and September.

Wildfires in California

Wildfires are a major hazard in southern California. Risks are greatest in late summer and autumn, and especially during periods of drought and prolonged high temperatures. Although wildfires caused by lightning strikes have always been a part of the natural ecosystem, 95% of wildfires in California today are due to people.

The frequency and intensity of wildfires increased in the 2007–09 drought (Figure 11.2). Five of the ten biggest wildfires ever recorded in California occurred between 2007 and 2009.

Impact

In 2008, wildfires in California burned around 520000ha of land and destroyed over 1000 structures. The economic cost to California was nearly US$900 million. Losses were also high in 2007, when nearly 4000 structures were destroyed. The 2009 fire season was less severe, although the cumulative effects of the three droughts meant that the first major wildfires occurred much earlier. In Santa Barbara County in May, a wildfire raged for 15 days, destroying 3500ha of forest and 80 homes. At its height it threatened the city of Santa Barbara, and one-third of the city's 90000 residents were evacuated (Figure 11.3, page 118). However, a much larger fire broke out on 26 August in the Angeles National Forest north of Pasadena. It destroyed 65000ha and 89 homes and killed two firemen. It took over 6 weeks to contain the blaze.

Exposure and vulnerability

Exposure to wildfires is high in southern California for a number of reasons. First, the hot, dry summers desiccate the vegetation, providing tinder-box conditions and abundant fuel for wildfires — conditions that become critical during long periods of drought. Second, there is the high density of population along the coast and in the foothills of the San Gabriel and San Bernardino mountains, where urban growth has encroached into parched scrubland, forests and woodland. And third, there are the Santa Ana winds.

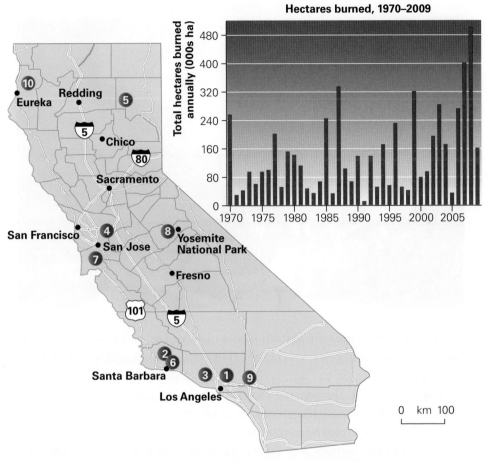

Figure 11.2   Wildfires in California: the ten largest fires in 2009

Fire name	County	Start	Contained	Hectares burned
1 Station	Los Angeles	26 August	16 October	64983
2 La Brea	Santa Barbara	8 August	22 August	36215
3 Guiberson	Ventura	22 September	27 September	7082
4 Corral	Alameda	13 August	16 August	4937
5 Hat Creek Complex	Shasta	1 August	12 August	4580
6 Jesusita	Santa Barbara	5 May	20 May	3534
7 Lockhead	Santa Cruz	12 August	23 August	3163
8 Big Meadow	Mariposa	26 August	10 September	3005
9 Sheep	San Bernardino	3 October	10 October	2833
10 Backbone	Trinity/Humboldt	1 July	24 July	2559

Figure
11.3 Smoke from the Jesusita fire fills the sky over houses in the Santa Barbara evacuation zone in May 2009

Cody Duncan/Alamy

The Santa Ana winds are easterlies that blow in autumn and early winter. They are hot, dry and gusty, and fan the flames of wildfires and spread embers. The winds develop on the southern edge of a large anticyclone centred over the Great Basin and the Mojave Desert (or High Desert) and blow towards low pressure over the Pacific Ocean. Because the Santa Ana winds originate at altitude, as they cross the coastal mountain ranges and descend to sea level they become even warmer and drier (relative humidity 10–20%). Funnelling of the winds through canyons and passes in the mountains increases their speed and gustiness and creates dangerous fire conditions (Figure 11.4).

Figure
11.4 Southern California's Santa Ana winds

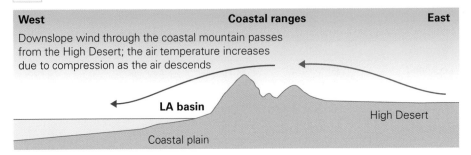

West   **Coastal ranges**   **East**

Downslope wind through the coastal mountain passes from the High Desert; the air temperature increases due to compression as the air descends

LA basin

High Desert

Coastal plain

Vulnerability to wildfires in California is mitigated by a highly trained professional fire service. In May 2009, at the height of the Santa Barbara fire, 3500 firefighters were called in to tackle the blaze. Following a major fire, disaster relief funding for up to 75% of firefighting costs is available from central government through FEMA. Even so, the task facing the fire services is so great that residents must also take responsibility for their own safety. Information published by local governments explains the fire risk and what people can do to help themselves. Many homes back onto natural areas like woodland and scrub, which pose significant risks. In these circumstances people are encouraged to clear vegetation around their homes to create a buffer zone. At the same time, homes within a 1.5 km radius of a natural area lie in the so-called 'ember zone' and are at risk from wind-driven embers. Residents here too need to take precautions. For instance, combustible building materials such as wood shingles for roofing might be replaced by tiles or slate. Meanwhile every household is advised to create a wildfire action plan that specifies evacuation routes, and provides fire extinguishers, hoses and emergency supplies.

Activity 1

Log on to the Ventura County website which deals with preparedness for wildfire disasters: **http://fire.countyofventura.org/Prevention/WildfirePreparedness/ tabid/231/Default.aspx**

Study the videos and other information on the site and describe what the public can do themselves to mitigate the threat from wildfires.

Heatwave in Europe: August 2003

An exceptional and prolonged heatwave struck much of Europe in summer 2003. The heatwave began in June and continued until mid-August. Large parts of the continent experienced temperatures that were 20–30% above the seasonal average. Historically, 2003 was the warmest summer in Europe since records began in 1755.

On 10 August, the UK recorded its highest-ever maximum temperature, 38.5 °C, with several weather stations in the Greater London area recording temperatures around 38 °C. At Gatwick in August, daily maximum temperatures exceeded 25 °C on ten successive days. Similar extremes were also recorded on the continent. In France, temperatures peaked at 40 °C and remained exceptionally high for 2 weeks; in Switzerland they rose to a record

41.5 °C on 11 August; and in southern Spain temperatures in excess of 40 °C occurred in most cities, reaching 46.2 °C in Cordoba and 45.2 °C in Seville.

The heatwave was caused by a stationary anticyclone anchored over western Europe, which blocked the intrusion of cooler air from the Atlantic (Figure 11.5). The situation was exceptional for two reasons: first, because of the extended period of time that the anticyclone remained stationary (20 days); and second, because the anticyclone generated a southerly airflow that drew in hot, dry tropical continental air (Tc) air from north Africa.

Figure 11.5 Synoptic chart: 8 August 2003

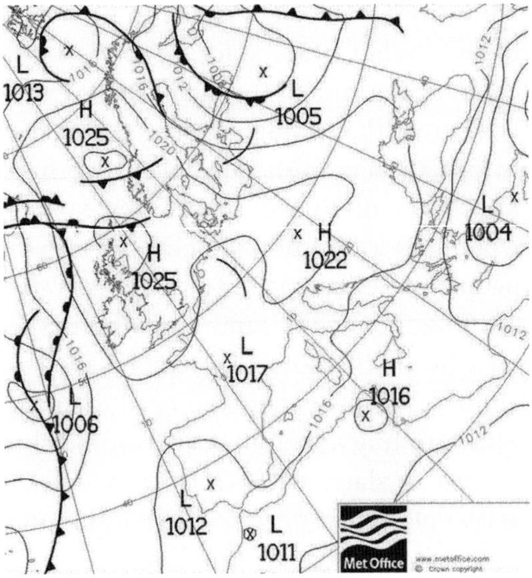

© Crown copyright (2003), the Met Office

Impact

The 2003 heatwave was responsible for the highest death toll of any natural hazard in Europe in the past 60 years. An estimated 30 000 excess deaths were attributed to the heatwave (Table 11.3). Worst hit was France, where the heatwave claimed some 14 000 lives. The big heat also caused high levels of mortality in Germany, Spain, Italy and the UK.

Extreme heat, especially in large urban areas, created a major health crisis (Figure 11.6). Elderly people were the most affected. In France, where the highest death rates were in the major cities, one-third of the excess deaths were in the Paris region, and 80% of the victims were aged 75 years and over.

The combination of excessive heat and drought had a severe impact on economic activities. The total costs to the EU were estimated to be around €10 billion. Agriculture was most badly affected. Extreme air temperatures and intense solar radiation from mid-July to mid-August resulted in high rates

Table 11.3 Estimated excess deaths due to the 2003 heatwave in Europe

France	14 082
Germany	7 000
Spain	4 200
Italy	4 000
UK	2 045
Netherlands	1 400
Portugal	1 300
Belgium	500

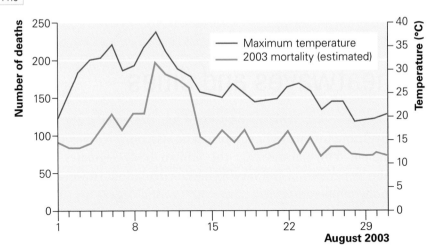

Figure 11.6 Maximum daily temperatures and mortality in London, August 2003

of evapotranspiration and excessive water consumption by crops. This created acute soil moisture deficits that lowered crop yields. Compared to 2002, wheat yields fell by 20% in France, 13% in Italy and 12% in the UK, while the total cereal harvest in the EU was down by 22 million tonnes. As well as this decline in the arable sector, outputs from livestock farming, of fodder crops and potatoes and wine production all fell steeply.

Low river levels meant that shipping was suspended on the rivers Elbe and Danube, and melting glaciers caused avalanches and flash floods in Switzerland. At Cologne, the River Rhine recorded its lowest flow since 1930. In France and Germany, river levels dropped so low that a number of nuclear power stations, reliant on river water for cooling, had to shut down. At the same time, demand for electricity soared as people switched on their air conditioning and adjusted the thermostats on their refrigerators.

The same combination of high temperatures and drought led to more than 25 000 wildfires. In total, nearly 650 000 ha of forest were destroyed. Portugal was the worst hit. There, 390 000 ha burned and 18 people were killed in the worst fire season for 23 years. In Spain, wildfires consumed 128 000 ha of forest. Other countries badly affected by wildfires included France, Austria, Finland, Denmark and Ireland.

Exposure and vulnerability

Extreme heatwaves like that of 2003 occur rarely in western Europe and in this respect exposure to heatwave hazards is low. On the other hand, when heatwaves do occur, the high density of population in western Europe puts millions at risk. Exposure is further increased because 80% of the population live in cities, which experience higher temperatures than rural areas. Risks are also increased by the fact that a large proportion of the people in western Europe are elderly (18% are aged 65 years and over).

Killer heatwaves and cities

The people most vulnerable to heatwaves are the elderly, the young, the chronically ill and urban dwellers. Normal human body temperature is 37 °C. When ambient temperatures rise, the human body regulates its internal temperature by perspiring and varying blood circulation. However, when the internal body temperature rises above 40 °C, vital organs are at risk. If the body temperature is not reduced, death follows. High humidity, which is a feature of western Europe's climate, makes extreme heat especially dangerous in that part of the world. In humid conditions there is little or no evaporation to cool the body and perspiration becomes ineffective.

Urban dwellers are particularly at risk during heatwaves. In summer, the difference in temperature between a large city such as London and the surrounding countryside can be as much as 10 °C. The reasons for high urban temperatures are as follows:

- Urban surfaces have low albedos, absorbing insolation during the day and creating a 'heat island' effect at night.
- Urban areas produce heat through domestic heating, factories and vehicles.
- There is a relative lack of vegetation cover, which through evapotranspiration would normally reduce temperatures.
- The lack of moisture in cities reduces evaporation (and therefore cooling), releasing more energy to heat the atmosphere.
- Apart from heat, people's bodies may be stressed by a pollution 'dome', which settles over cities during spells of anticyclonic weather.

The UK's big chill: cold spell 2009–10

The cold weather that began in mid-December 2009 and extended to mid-January 2010 was the longest spell of severe winter weather in the UK since 1963, the coldest winter of the twentieth century. At Manchester, the average daily temperature between 17 December 2009 and 9 January 2010 was –2.5 °C (Figure 11.7). In a 25-day period, frost was recorded on 23 days, with a minimum temperature of –15 °C on 7 January. A combination of clear skies, arctic air and a snow cover caused temperatures to plunge to –22.3 °C at Altnaharra in Scotland on 8 January, while minimum temperatures below –10 °C were common as far south as southern England. On 8 January, the temperature in the city centre in Edinburgh at 07.00 was just –11 °C. Between 4 and 9 January, in many parts of the UK, sub-zero temperatures prevailed all day, and snow lay continuously for over 3 weeks. Heavy snowfalls blanketed most of the country (Figure 11.8) with up to 21 cm falling in Hampshire on 5 January.

The cold weather continued throughout February, with temperatures 1–2 °C below average for the month. Overall the winter of 2009–10 (November to February) was the coldest since 1978–79.

Prolonged cold spells in western Europe are usually associated with blocking anticyclones. The 2009–10 cold spell was no exception. The North Atlantic Oscillation (NAO) switched into a negative phase and remained there for most of December and January. High pressure from eastern Europe and Siberia extended westwards, flooding western Europe with freezing arctic and

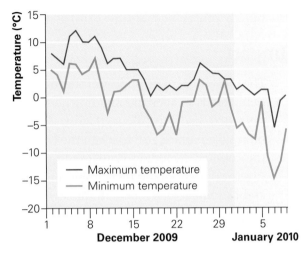

Figure 11.7 Maximum and minimum daily temperatures at Manchester: 2 December 2009–9 January 2010

Figure 11.8 NASA satellite image of snow-covered UK, 7 January 2010

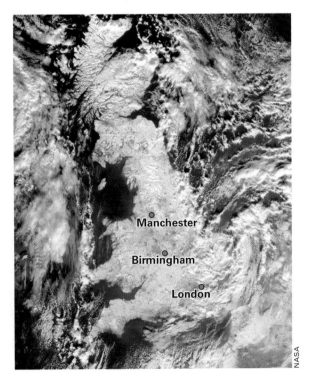

polar air. The polar front jet stream shifted south, diverting major Atlantic storms into Iberia and the Mediterranean. This part of Europe experienced unusually wet and stormy weather. The normal mild westerly circulation over the UK broke down, to be replaced by northerly and easterly flows bringing bitterly cold arctic maritime (Am) and polar continental (Pc) air masses.

Impact

The most immediate impact of the 'big chill' was the disruption of transport. Many roads in Scotland and northern England were closed. Side roads were untreated and hazardous (Figure 11.9), and motorists were stranded in blizzard conditions on roads in the Highlands and Pennines. Airports across the country, including Gatwick, Bristol, Manchester, Leeds, Liverpool and Inverness, were closed for variable lengths of time, with many flights delayed and cancelled. High-speed train services through the Channel Tunnel were suspended for several days (around Christmas) as trains were unable to cope with snow on the continent. Several broke down in the tunnel, resulting in long queues of passengers at St Pancras station. Deliveries of food to supermarkets became increasingly difficult, and in rural areas milk collections were suspended and thousands of litres of milk poured away. By early January, around 10 000 schools had closed, and absenteeism from work reached 10%,

Figure 11.9 Difficult driving conditions in the Pennines, January 2010

Ian Dagnell/Alamy

costing the UK economy nearly £700 million a day. Gas supplies to major industrial users were reduced on 7 January and there were fears that gas and electricity suppliers might not be able to meet record demand. Bin collection was suspended as side roads became impassable. Although 200 000 tonnes of rock salt were spread on roads to keep traffic moving, by early January supplies began to run out. Production of salt from the UK's two mines in Cheshire was unable to keep pace with demand. Sport was badly disrupted. Premier League football, rugby matches and race meetings were cancelled, often for reasons of health and safety of spectators rather than because of frozen ground. Accident and emergency units in hospitals were overwhelmed by the huge numbers of minor injuries. By 10 January, 27 deaths were blamed on the cold spell, due mainly to icy roads, avalanches and hypothermia.

Exposure and vulnerability

Levels of exposure to extreme winter weather lasting more than a week are relatively low in the UK. In the past 60 years, notable cold spells only occurred in 1947, 1963, 1979 and 1981. The normal pattern of winter weather is dominated by westerly, oceanic influences, with average maximum daily temperatures around 7 or 8 °C and minimum temperatures above freezing on most nights.

However, when a long cold spell becomes established, it causes widespread economic disruption. This is because the UK's vulnerability to cold weather is high. The reason is that levels of preparedness are relatively low. Because cold spells occur infrequently, investment in snow-clearing machinery and stockpiles of rock salt are limited. There is no political will to raise taxes and prepare for extreme winter weather that occurs on average only once every 25 years. The same is true for individual households. Few motorists invest in snow tyres for their vehicles because in most winters they are not needed. Compared to countries such as Finland and Sweden, where severe winters are common events, long cold spells have a disproportionate impact in the UK. Even relatively minor snowfalls have the potential to cause chaos and bring traffic to a standstill.

Response

Local highway agencies have some snow-clearing equipment and salt the roads when ground temperatures are forecast to fall below freezing. International airports also invest in snow-clearing machines, and railway operators heat points to avoid icing. The Met Office issues severe weather warnings to the public and local authorities for snow and ice, often advising against travel unless essential. Television channels and local radio stations broadcast weather forecasts and advice on travel. Winter fuel payments from government help pensioners to heat their homes: additional payments to the poorest pensioners are triggered following 7 successive days of sub-zero mean temperatures.

Activity 2

Research and write an account of the UK winter 2009–10, the coldest for over 30 years. Include (a) detailed statistics of temperatures, frost and snowfall; (b) regional variations in the severity of winter weather; (c) the economic and social impact of the extreme weather.

As a starting point, refer to the Met Office and the *Guardian* websites:

www.metoffice.gov.uk/corporate/pressoffice/2010/pr20100301.html

www.guardian.co.uk/uk/2010/mar/02/british-winter-coldest-30-years